Wide Open Spaces

Wide Open Spaces

Women Exploring Call

Through Stories and Reflections

Edited by

Carol Henderson

Hampshire, England
Cleveland, Ohio

First published by Circle Books, 2011
Circle Books is an imprint of John Hunt Publishing Ltd., The Bothy, Deershot Lodge, Park Lane,
Ropley, Hants, SO24 0BE, UK
office1@o-books.net
www.o-books.com

For distributor details and how to order please visit the 'Ordering' section on our website.

Text copyright: Carol D. Henderson 2010

ISBN: 978 1 84694 563 2

A CIP catalogue record for this book is available from the British Library.

Design: Stuart Davies

Printed in the UK by CPI Antony Rowe
Printed in the USA by Offset Paperback Mfrs, Inc

CONTENTS

Editor, Carol Henderson
Contributors: Liz Dowling-Sendor, Marilyn Hein,
Marcia Mount Shoop, Nancy Rozak, Judy Stephens,
Caroline Craig Proctor, Betty Berghaus, Katie Ricks,
Cely Chicurel, Debbie Kirk, Judith S. Stephens,
Susan Steinberg

Acknowledgments

This book is the fruit of many seeds, planted and nurtured by an abundance of grace and labor. We are grateful to Louis B. Weeks, President Emeritus of Union Presbyterian Seminary in Richmond and Charlotte, who understood that the Church's field of leaders needed tending and developed The Rehoboth Project as a result. Our gratefulness also extends to The Rehoboth Project Steering Committee, which supported the concept of a women-only group and approved a second round of funding for us to complete the essays included in the pages that follow. Carol Henderson, writing coach, editor and friend, inspired us to delve more deeply into our call stories; without Carol's prompts, we would not have written the first word. We are thankful to our families, friends and congregations, who granted us the time to explore wide open spaces, sustained us in varying ways throughout the writing process, and assisted us as we pruned our narratives. Cely Chicurel invited us into her home and prepared her table for us each month; we were all touched and blessed by her boundless and artful hospitality. It's hard to know how to thank Susan Steinberg; her guiding vision, hard work, and generosity made our Rehoboth group a reality. Above all, we give thanks and praise to God, who planted the seed of faith within each of us and beyond all our imagining made room for our faith to grow.

Editor's Note

The first time I met with the Rehoboth group, I felt like a bit of a kill-joy when it was time to get started. The women were standing around in groups, chatting and laughing. Clearly they loved this monthly chance to get together. I hated to break up the party—for writing.

They had no idea what to expect from this session. I was introduced as the author of the book they had in front of them, a memoir about my son's death and my struggles with grief. Was this going to be like a book club, hosting a visiting author? I'm sure they were wondering if they were going to have to suffer through my talking about the process of writing the book, and then ask pertinent questions. Too often, in their professional lives as ministers and educators, these women had to deal with the grief and suffering of others. In fact one woman told me she had to leave early that day to give a memorial service. The last thing they needed was to focus on me, my writing life, my grief story.

I told the women right away that this was a workshop and it was for them. I wasn't going to talk about writing a memoir. They were going to write, for and about themselves, and if they felt inclined, share their writing with the group. I assured them there were no rules for this writing, no right or wrong way to approach the prompts. No one was going to correct their grammar or their ideas. "Write about whatever bubbles up and catches your attention," I said. "Write about what poet Allen Ginsberg called, 'first thought.' Try not to censor yourselves. Let it rip."

Then I gave them the first prompt: "What matters?"

Many of the women looked at me, confused.

"Write about what matters to you," I said. "Right here, right now. What's on your mind? What are you thinking about?"

They bowed their heads and wrote, and so began our journey of working together. The women welcomed the chance to examine, through writing, their own inner landscapes—without feeling pressure to produce a sermon, respond to a congregant, generate curriculum, edit a newsletter article, or research a theological paper. They liked being jostled out of their comfortable patterns of thinking and writing. They saw firsthand how deep reflective writing can take us places within ourselves we would not otherwise go—and that, as writing begets writing, meaning grows on the page.

I was able to work with each woman individually. In almost every private meeting, the women told me important, sometimes essential, aspects of their lives they had considered writing about but shied away from in their essays.

"Write about that," I would say, again and again. "Others will identify with your trials and appreciate your honesty. Write about what makes you sweat and feel faint. Write about what's really important."

Prompt-driven free writes began to grow into essay drafts. The women expanded, revised and rewrote—honing their early drafts into tight narratives of their personal call stories. Each of the essays—they range between nine and twenty-seven pages—is as individual in style and tone as the women who wrote them; the qualities that shine through are grittiness, doubt, candor, bravery, and the determination to follow their spiritual paths.

The women talk eloquently about vulnerability, discrimination, betrayal, and the many burdens and joys of their chosen calls. They discuss Sabbath, grace, "burn-out," and conflict (both personal and institutional).

We hope you'll have many "Oh, yes. I know just how she feels" moments as you read—and that magical things will happen for you when you put pen to paper. Writing clarifies muddled thought, helps us make meaningful connections. When we dig down for what's buried inside and give it voice on the page, we can then observe it, play with it, revise and reconsider it. Writing can transform us.

In the Afterword, you'll find several of the prompts I used with the women. We hope you'll try some of them. You'll also find guidelines for leading a reflective writing group as well as some of our favorite memoirs about call and books about the writing process.

Don't hesitate to be in touch. We'd love to hear from you about your experience with *Wide Open Spaces*. To contact us: www.carolhenderson.com

Introduction

The book of Genesis tells us that when Isaac established himself in the valley of Gerar, he had trouble finding water. His servants re-dug two wells from Abraham's time, but the local people objected, saying that the water was theirs. Finally Isaac found a place to dig a well that no one else claimed. He named it Rehoboth, "wide or free spaces; room for us."

Isaac's search resonates with many of us who have felt God's call and sought to respond. As fulfilling as we find ministry and church life, there are times when conflict consumes us, uncertainty about our place fills us with doubt, and exhaustion leaves our spirits and bodies parched. We travel too far without renewal and find ourselves alone, thirsting for the refreshing water only God can provide.

Wide Open Spaces is an offering of reflections on calling by eleven women whose cups were replenished by God under the auspices of The Rehoboth Project. A Sustaining Pastoral Excellence peer support initiative, The Rehoboth Project was designed by Union Theological Seminary and the Presbyterian School of Christian Education, and funded by the Religion Division of Lilly Endowment.

We describe this collection as an offering because the opportunity to write was a gift, and our faith tells us that gifts are for sharing. The process of writing was so meaningful to us that we did not want to keep the experience to ourselves. Each of our essays is followed by prompts to spark your own exploration of God's call, and there are further suggestions at the end. We hope these resources lead you, too, to a wide open space, where the well runs deep.

Our Rehoboth group first met in January, 2006. We began by choosing a mug from a colorful selection made by one of our leaders, Cely Chicurel, a master potter. "Hold the empty cup in your hands," Joyce Rupp writes in *The Cup of Our Life*, the devotional resource we chose to open each meeting. "Let the emptiness remind you of your yearnings. Be thirsty for God."

We looked into our empty cups and then one by one we told our stories. As we put the peaks and valleys of our call journeys into words, our cups began to fill. We moved from isolation into newfound community. A sacred trust held us close. God's grace was a palpable presence around the table, assuring us that we had been led to the right well.

We met at Cely's house once a month for prayer, conversation and renewal. In one of our first sessions, Cely taught us how to make our own cups; we each had a turn at the potter's wheel. At another meeting we learned about spiritual direction, at another we discussed healing prayer with a parish nurse, and at another we explored what it means to "preach from the center." Every meeting had a different theme, and yet the same purpose: to refresh our cups from a wide open space.

Each guest we invited to join us left us with new insights and inspiration. But writing coach Carol Henderson stood out. Her writing prompts led us in directions we had not taken, places we had not been. When we shared what we had written in response to the questions "What do you carry?" and "Where are you from?" we laughed and cried and longed for more. Carol taught us how to deepen our cups and then fill them, too.

After several more gatherings with Carol we decided to delve yet more deeply. Eleven of us agreed to write about our experience of God's call, and with the generous support of The Rehoboth Project we had the gift of Carol's wisdom and expertise to guide us. Carol pushed us, graciously, to tell the truth. She gave us evocative prompts and asked us more questions. She edited our essays and patiently waited for our revisions.

When the essays were done, we read them out loud to the group. As at our very first meeting several years earlier, God's grace enveloped the room. Often there was a long and holy pause when the readers of the day were finished. We always closed our time together with a prayer of thanksgiving for what we had been privileged to hear.

Once again, God drew us from isolation into community. Opening up to each other, being vulnerable to the pain and the joy of our call stories, we saw one of the great affirmations of our faith confirmed: we are not alone. Carol knew what she was doing when she urged us to be honest.

Though we had known each other for three years, the writing brought new truths to the surface. "Church was home for me," writes Katie Ricks. Yet when she came out as a lesbian in early adulthood, that home-like feeling of welcome, comfort and blessing changed dramatically. Marilyn Hein describes how her calling into ministry was denied by those who told her that women could not be pastors. After years of searching for the path that best suited her, Judy Stephens was exhilarated when the way opened for her to become an ordained Deacon in the United Methodist Church. Yet when she went back to her home church to share her excitement and offer her ministry, her pastor told her there was no place for her there.

Most of us have gone through seasons of broken trust. Several of us are survivors of sexual violations. Our faith has also been tested by deep loss—death, divorce, and disease. Football and fire have altered the courses of our lives and influenced our relationships with God. We are also well acquainted with doubt and uncertainty about our callings. For some of us, motherhood threw everything into question. We struggled to find the elusive balance between family life and professional life and waited in vain to hear clear instructions from above. We pushed ourselves to the limit, sometimes with very little compensation, striving to earn our salvation from a Jesus whose boundless grace we proclaimed and taught every week. We wondered, as Caroline Craig Proctor says, about the meaning of our black robes and our place in the Church. But as Marcia Mount Shoop writes, "God keeps gently offering unlikely moments of clarity."

Rehoboth gave us a wide open space to name those moments, to affirm one another's worth, and to see the connections between what seemed like disparate parts of our own stories. In ways beyond our own imagining, God has guided us along our various atypical paths. We have felt blessed.

Our hope is that these narratives will be a blessing to you, as you explore your own calling. We invite you to respond to the prompts at the end of each essay by yourself, in your own journal, or with a trusted group. However you proceed, in Carol's words, let yourself go deep; or as the author Maryanne Radmacher says, "lean forward into your life." Write and write and then look for what is hidden in the space between the words. God only knows what treasures you will find.

Stretching, Struggling, Rejoicing

Liz Dowling-Sendor

My first impression of God was as sunlight. I was about three or four, and – because no one in Beaufort, South Carolina in the mid-1950s had central heating in the winter — I was huddled by the fireplace. I had found a patch of sun in which to sit. It warmed me. I closed my eyes and looked up, feeling goldenness on my face. Somehow I made the connection: That's God, right there. That's God's love pouring over me.

When I was six and visiting my mother's family in England, I found God again. My mother and I had hiked up a hill covered with buttercups. Their yellow heads nodded and shone at us in the sunlight, lining our way. At the top, all by itself in this expanse of green and gold, stood a small stone church. I picked one tiny flower before we entered the cool darkness of the nave. At the altar, I placed my flower in a small glass and knelt. And I felt something that I can only describe as an enlarging, and warming, in my heart. God's presence, at that place, at that moment, surrounding and filling us.

It might sound improbable for a young child to be thinking so much about God. But God, or at least Church, animated the story of my family. Both sides were proud Baptists. My mother, from Lancashire, England, talked about her great-grandfather who was a Baptist minister and even gave his son the middle name of "Baptist." "And that's *your* great-grandfather, Henry Baptist Bury," she'd say, showing me a fading photograph of a round, cheery man with a brushy moustache, holding a little blonde girl – my mother – on his lap.

My great-grandfather on my father's side, William Hamilton Dowling, served as a Baptist chaplain in the Civil War and rode circuit afterward to tiny congregations across the South

Carolina Low Country. He died long before I was born, but I felt connected to him through my father's stories about his sense of humor and his powerful, and memorably *long*, sermons. The Dowling Family Reunion, which we attended without fail every year, occurred on the Sunday nearest his August 4 birthday and took place at Hopewell Baptist Church, where he preached his first and last sermons. After the fried-chicken dinner on the grounds, we would stand in the white gravel of the cemetery and gaze at his grave.

My parents and older brothers and I attended the local Baptist church. It was a formidable edifice — you entered by climbing a set of wide stairs and walking through fat white columns. And from what I could see, you only entered if you were white. Even as a girl, I struggled to sort out the two theologies the church presented. In Sunday school I found the God I had met in the sunlight by the fireplace and at the altar in England – warm, inviting, loving. The teachers, all women, were as simple and sweet as the orange Kool-aid and Hydrox cookies they offered to help us get through the long morning. I wrote in my diary one afternoon at age nine, "When I went into Sunday school today, I, well, something felt like it was carrying me on my feet. It was a funny feeling."

At the worship service, however, another God showed up – a God angry about our sin and depravity. The preacher frightened me. His voice would drop to a whisper, then unexpectedly explode in a shout that made me jump. I remember sermons about our faith and actions being inadequate, that we might be headed for damnation. The sermons lasted about forty-five minutes – I counted out each minute on my father's watch as I sat beside him in the pew. I wrote in my diary, "I think he's like the preacher in *Pollyanna*. He tends to look on the dark side. I wish he could find joy in God and Christ."

My weekly immersion in church prompted me to pray about everything. I prayed for my little black kitten Moe to return (he

did, but with a tumor on his neck, and he died shortly afterwards), for no snakes to cross in front of me on the path to the
beach (only one did, after the first snake which prompted the
prayers), for me to be able to forgive my brother and for him to
forgive me despite the fact that we fought every day. I wrote in
my diary: "How can we love each other? ... I don't know what
God thinks of me. What can I do?" At age ten, I wrote: "I've
decided to become a missionary-nurse. I'd like to work with
people and help them, and I'd truly love to spread Jesus' and
God's love to them."

Around this time, church members started to pressure me to
be baptized. I resisted. Although I felt God's love for me, I did
not like the church's emphasis on baptism as "submission" to
Jesus. The idea of baptism as sudden, helpless capitulation
didn't seem to have anything to do with my sense of God as
gently guiding and supporting. My parents went along with me:
my mother had never been baptized, and my father said he
remembered feeling pressured into baptism at my age. When
church people came from the Wednesday-night prayer meeting
to talk to me, my parents politely but firmly told them I wasn't
interested.

In 1962, when I was ten, my mother started going to the
Episcopal church. Her father in England – Grandpa, of the
merry blue eyes and smile – had died. She chose to talk about
her grief with the quiet, unassuming priest at St. Helena's. The
beauty of the Episcopal liturgy helped her, too. She was a poet,
and she felt a resonance with the flowing words of praise and
prayer. She was baptized at St. Helena's one afternoon, with just
my father and us three kids attending.

I started attending services with her at that graceful 18th-
century church. I loved the intimacy, the peace of the place. I,
too, loved the liturgy, its rhythms and images beating so closely
with the impulses of my heart. I loved the priest's rich voice,
rising and falling on the words of the service, a voice charged

with compassion and celebration. He was unpretentious, almost shy, outside church. But during services his voice became transformed, filled. His hands lovingly consecrated bread and wine. I began to long to feel God's power in my voice and in my hands, God's blessing flowing through me to those around me. I would imagine myself somehow in the priest's place, saying those words, making those gestures with my hands. I knew, however, that no girl, no woman, could do such a thing.

At one Good Friday service, while I was kneeling and trying to imagine the suffering of Christ (I was likening it to the suffering my brother and I imposed on each other, knowing also that wasn't quite it), I felt the presence, almost the person, of Jesus coming in the side door nearby and kneeling with me in the pew. He seemed so gentle. A sensation of complete comfort washed over me. My mother gave me *The Book of Common Prayer* for my eleventh birthday. "Religion has taken on a new meaning now," I wrote. "And with God, my prayer book, and my Bible to guide me, it will be the dearest thing in my life, except for my family."

Looking back, those words sound unimaginably pious. The truth is, no one would've guessed I wrote them. As I entered my teen years, I was into clothes, boys, being popular, and sneaking off to drink cheap wine from the 7-11. I felt pressure – not from my parents, but from within myself – to get good grades and look beautiful. To offset the stress, I'd drive out to the beach and run off my nervous energy, then sit and watch undulations of waves and clouds. Sometimes I would remember how it felt to experience God's presence. One night when I was a senior, I felt strangely compelled to get out pen and paper. I found myself writing on into the night about God's love and the importance of loving other people, energized by a power and vibrancy I hadn't felt for years.

Then I went to college. At Harvard, it took no time for my classmates to destroy any sense of my superiority. Everyone seemed, and probably was, more intelligent, sophisticated and accomplished. Certainly more worldly-wise. I widened my eyes at breakfast on my second morning when a girl across the table picked up what looked to me like a stale, hard doughnut. She sliced it horizontally, then slathered it with cream cheese. A sliced Krispy Kreme with cream cheese? I was shocked. As she opened her mouth to eat, she caught my gaze. "What," she asked, "you never saw a bagel before?"

A few days later, when I went biking, I tossed into the basket behind me the hand-tooled leather handbag that my English grandmother had made. It held my wallet, bank card, and family photos. Coming from Beaufort, South Carolina, I didn't realize this was not the safest place to put a handbag. Stopped at a light in Harvard Square, I felt a slight movement of the bike and looked around. The handbag was gone. My parents were traveling and couldn't be reached. I knew no one. I didn't even remember to cry out to God. Instead, I shuddered into a sense of loneliness and displacement that lasted for much of that year.

The next fall, I moved from my huge freshman dormitory to a small house where nine other women were living. I don't think I ever attended a church service during college, but those women were church for me. We laughed and baked and sang and partied together, and buoyed each other up when we sank down. Academically, I had expected to major in religion, to try to explore what this "God" stuff of my youth was all about. But Harvard at the time (I heard it was due to a "curriculum cleansing" decades before) offered no religion major. So I majored in art history and sneaked in religion by studying the art and architecture of that God-infused era, the Middle Ages.

As graduation approached, I started getting nervous about a job. I had spent a semester as a student curator at the Whitney Museum of American Art in New York, weighing the idea of museum work. But the fast-paced, ego-centered art world didn't feel right. I didn't want to go to graduate school; scholars seemed too isolated from the real world. An older journalist friend in Cambridge urged me to go home and be a reporter. "Save the world!" he urged. "Write about real people, real things." I got a job on a weekly paper in Hilton Head Island, South Carolina, then moved up to the daily in Beaufort, then eventually to newspapers in Charlotte, Washington, D.C., and Raleigh, North Carolina.

What I loved most about journalism, besides getting to meet interesting people, was the writing. Language stands in my mind like a medieval cathedral, its power and subtlety both reflecting and beckoning us toward something divine. To me, writing can be prayer. The process is mysterious and holy: just the right word arises, sentences take on rhythm; themes emerge and begin to recur. As both the creator and recipient of these events, I witness the whole story ripple into place, and a holy pleasure starts to shine within me.

I often felt like a misfit as a journalist, though. I liked interviewing people, but I realized I wasn't there to befriend or help them, but to get five good quotes and a slew of facts and head back to the office to file the story on deadline. I grew tired of the reporter's disease – cynicism – brought on by the job of uncovering society's flaws but not working directly to correct them. I found I'd caught the affliction too.

In 1977 I moved from being a reporter at *The Charlotte Observer* to editing and writing for a magazine in New York. I reconnected with Ben, a friend from college. As our relationship evolved, it didn't seem to matter at first that he was Jewish and I, or at least my background, was Christian. I'd hardly gone to church in years. Ben hadn't been serious about Judaism either, and, as he told it, his parents, who were Conservative Jews, usually only attended High Holiday services and were casual about keeping kosher.

We talked about having one religion in the family if we were to marry. Ben felt his Jewish heritage ruled out his converting to

Christianity – plus he worried his parents and particularly his brother, who had become an Orthodox rabbi, would disapprove. I thought I might be able to hold onto my beliefs about God if I became Jewish. We started going to a Conservative synagogue in New York, where the assistant rabbi, Alvin, kept us entertained with such lines as "I'm a strict vegetarian – *except* for corned beef." I struggled for months over the decision to convert to Judaism. One afternoon, I went to St. Patrick's Cathedral on Fifth Avenue to try to discern some message from God. As I sat alone in a pew, I asked God, What should I do? I heard nothing. I decided all I could do was go forward with the conversion.

Two weeks before our wedding, we walked to the conversion ceremony on Manhattan's Lower East Side. I had plenty of time to feel troubled that I was about to become Jewish, that it somehow wasn't *me*. I told Ben about my misgivings, but we walked on. At the *mikveh*, the ritual bath, a tiny old Russian woman with a mouthful of silver teeth met me. She instructed me to immerse myself three times and say three blessings in Hebrew, which I was to repeat after her. Three Orthodox rabbis stood on the other side of a wall, listening to the water splashings and the words to make sure I was doing everything correctly.

I immersed myself once, then twice, then three times. As I came up for the third and final time, it seemed like the ceiling of the room opened up. I could almost hear a voice, a loving voice, saying something that surrounded me and lifted me with love, that seemed to suggest I was God's child, among God's children. The effect on me was physical. I was shocked, confused, transported, ecstatic. I felt, more strongly and surely than ever, the powerful, the overwhelming presence of God.

I was so moved by my experience in the *mikveh* that I started sorting out what it meant in my life. After our wedding, at which Rabbi Alvin officiated, I wanted to play a greater part in his synagogue, to join a community, to be God's child among

God's children. We observed the Sabbath by walking to and from services every Friday night and Saturday morning. I learned to sing in Hebrew and went up to the *bimah* to chant the prayers before and after the rabbi read from the Torah. I carried the Torah through the congregation as people touched it for a blessing. We attended Talmud and *midrash* studies led by Rabbi Alvin.

Despite my involvement, I realized after a while that I didn't feel comfortable at the synagogue. For one thing, I could not blend in. My blonde hair and blue eyes broadcast the fact I was what some call a "shiksa" (a derogatory term for a Gentile girl). But I was also uncomfortable theologically. The liturgy seemed not to emphasize what had drawn me to Christianity – the idea of the unconditional, unearned grace of God's love; the possibility of experiencing an intimate contact with God. Services began to leave me spiritually empty.

One October weekend when we were visiting Harvard, we attended the Quaker meeting with friends. It was a perfect fall morning in New England; the sharp light and bright colors ignited in me a fiery sense of joy. This was my first Friends meeting, but I caught on that the idea was to wait to see if God touched your heart, and then say what you felt moved to say. Since I was a novice, I fully expected to remain quiet and observe. But a few minutes into the meeting, as others stood and spoke, my heart started thumping and my body actually started trembling. I had to hold my hands under the pew to stay seated. A long silence opened up. No one stood and spoke. I realized it was somehow my turn to speak, almost as if they were all waiting for me. I stood and uttered some words about the beauty of the day, then sat down. The trembling stopped. But I was shaken to the marrow.

I felt I had rediscovered intimate contact with God. We attended Friends meetings in New York and, when we moved to Washington, D.C. in 1979, we attended Friends meetings there.

The hour-long discipline of listening for the guidance of God, and sometimes being called to respond, connected me back to the warming sunlight on my face as a child, the hushed stone church in the field of buttercups.

I was now experiencing similar feelings at another location – the Washington Cathedral. It was only a block from our apartment. On my walks there, I reveled in the lavender shadows of the nave, watched the rose windows change color with the sun's movement through the day, and soaked up the peace of the Bishop's Garden. One day while wandering the grounds, I came upon the Shalem Institute, a center for spiritual direction. I signed up to meet with a spiritual director who helped me try to understand my experiences with God and discern what God was now calling me to do. I found myself telling her I had once wanted to be an Episcopal priest and that those feelings were returning. But that seemed laughable: I had never been baptized. Plus, I was an Orthodox Jew. Occasionally, then more frequently, I attended an Episcopal church on Capitol Hill with a friend from the magazine where I worked.

We moved to Raleigh so I could take a job at the newspaper. We continued attending Quaker meetings; I also went by myself to an Episcopal church. At one point I talked to the priest there about the spiritual diversity of our Jewish-Quaker-Episcopal marriage. He suggested, "Maybe there are some things in life that just don't get resolved." The wisdom of his words, the idea that we could follow an unusual religious path and trust God despite the ambiguity, gave me some peace.

Meanwhile, my misgivings about journalism grew. I badly hurt my back one spring by picking up a pile of newspapers (the irony wasn't lost on me). After a few weeks of healing in bed, mulling over what I was doing with my life, I decided to quit the paper, get work from magazine editors I knew, and start freelancing.

A year later, in 1985, our daughter Julia was born. I loved her passionately from the moment we looked into each other's eyes. But, never having cared for infants, I hadn't expected the abundance of work and the absence of sleep. I had never given myself up totally to another person. I found it hard to summon that kind of devotion, yet I had to. One evening I got down on my knees, exhausted, and asked God to grant me the energy and patience I needed to care for her. I felt love pouring down on me; I felt the strength come into me to be a mother, a nurturer. In the days and weeks afterwards, I got better at caring for her and comforting her, and I began to feel my arms around her as being, when *I* despaired, like God's arms around me.

We moved to Chapel Hill in 1986. One day, when I was talking to a friend who worked as a career counselor, she asked me, "If you were on your death bed right now, what would you regret you hadn't done in your life?" I immediately blurted out, "Become an Episcopal priest." I laughed; of course, that was impossible for an un-baptized Orthodox Jew. Besides, pursuing the priesthood might create emotional strain on Ben and me. But my friend didn't laugh. "You had a lot of energy when you said that," she pointed out. "You need to at least take the idea seriously."

After the sadness of a miscarriage the next December, we bought a Christmas tree for our house and a little angel to put on top. Her smile and outstretched arms were soothing. Then astonishment replaced sorrow when I discovered, a few months later, that I was expecting twins. The doctor said they might well be born too early. Julia had come a month early, and that was only one baby. I spent my days rotating between worrying and praying for strength. When I went into labor eleven weeks early, my doctor put me on complete bed rest. I spent six weeks lying still and counting off the days, one by one, trying to trust. In the end, William and Adam were born healthy and only about a month early. My relief and love for them felt like rich colors surging inside me. One Sunday morning soon after they were born, I went to the Episcopal church down the street, saw my obstetrician there, and exulted, "There are miracles all around us!" Smiling, he agreed.

I had joined the local Mothers of Twins Club when I learned I was carrying twins. The women there were fun-loving, strong and sympathetic. And honest. We discouraged any pretence of perfection or flawlessness; instead, we felt free to confess how difficult life could be and how inadequate we often felt. When my boys were past infancy, I began to get calls from other mothers who needed someone to listen to their struggles, and I felt honored to be invited into those difficult parts of their lives. During the year I was president of the club, I wrote monthly newsletter essays about the joys and challenges of having twins. I called them my "sermons" without realizing what impact they were having on me.

On Sunday mornings we occasionally attended the local Friends meetings or I visited different Episcopal churches. One morning I drove past the Friends meeting to check out the Church of the Holy Family, a small Episcopal Church near the shopping mall. From the opening hymn, I felt at home there. The music and the people seemed filled with the kind of spirit of God's grace I had experienced before.

When I went to talk with Timothy, the rector, who had recently arrived there himself, I admitted that the priesthood had been a childhood dream. But I repeated, as always, that goal would be impossible to pursue, given that I was an un-baptized Jew and reluctant to impose the burden of Christian ordination on my marriage. He listened intently; I felt he understood my frustration. And I noticed something else: he did not overtly agree with me that the priesthood was out of the question.

When the twins were eighteen months old, I leaned down to pick up one of them and tore a ligament on my spine. I could hardly move for weeks. I scrambled to arrange full-time childcare. I tried to allay my anxiety by tracking my recovery –

how many more minutes and then hours I could remain standing each day. Then I sneezed and tore the ligament again. My trust in healing collapsed. If a simple sneeze could disable me, I might never get well. One night when I was especially scared, I began to pray to Jesus to lift me from my hopelessness. I felt I saw him appear at a half-open door. The image gave me a sense of utter peace that God's love was with me. Over the next six months, I did gradually heal.

That vision of Jesus, coupled with my desire to join the community I had found at Holy Family, led me toward baptism. I told Ben I didn't expect him to follow suit. And we assured each other that we would continue to talk about how we could pursue our spiritual path together.

Timothy scheduled my baptism for the Great Vigil of Easter. That year, the vigil also fell on the first night of Passover. We took the kids to a seder at a friend's house. I felt disoriented – here I was participating as a Jew in the central festival of Judaism, then heading off to become a Christian in the central festival of Christianity. After the seder, I drove alone in the dark to Holy Family. I sat by myself in the pew. When it came time for the baptism, I walked forward, shaking, and stood by a man who held a baby girl in a white gown. What I remember most was her tiny bare foot pointed toward me, pink and pure. Timothy poured water over my head, handed me a towel, and did the same for the baby. As I found my way back to the pew, a parishioner called out, "Welcome to the family."

The congregation soon felt like family. I taught adult Sunday School, served communion, visited the sick and shut-in, led prayer services, and served meals on a team at the homeless shelter. Even so, my own nuclear family always came first. On Sundays, when we would read the words of the post-communion prayer, "Send us out to do the work you have given us to do," an image of my children would spontaneously arise as my "work." They were teaching me patience, moderation, and self-effacement – qualities I needed in my vocation as a mother.

Always in the back of my mind, though, lay the question of ordination. Timothy hadn't ruled it out. After a while, when I prayed the post-communion prayer, what increasingly came to mind was an image of preaching and celebrating the Eucharist.

In May 1992 I wrote, "I've often heard that writers know they are really writers because they can't imagine doing anything else but writing. That's how I feel about ordination. I know I won't be at peace until I at least try to go forward."

Meanwhile, to both of our surprise, Ben had a strong spiritual experience of his own and decided to be baptized. He became actively involved at Holy Family. That summer we took the kids to an Episcopal retreat center in western North Carolina. One afternoon I entered the chapel, walked to the front, and gazed for a while at the stained-glass window. I fixed my eyes on Jesus' face. As I turned back toward the altar, I felt Jesus' gaze on me. At the altar, I stopped. I felt something rush through me, a feeling that I belonged there. I found myself stretching out my arms and lifting them in prayer as a priest would, and at that moment I felt a prickly sensation on my hands. My body felt weightless. Then I went up into the pulpit and looked out over the empty pews. I had a sensation of being suspended halfway between heaven and earth, of receiving something from heaven to give to earth.

I had a similar experience leading a service of Morning Prayer. As I said the words of the service, I felt something shaping my voice and the rhythm of my speech. I felt the words on the page of the prayer book illuminated as I read them. I felt my heartbeat racing, a light within me, and a sense that the light was spreading to others around me. I felt ready to explode with joy. I knew it was time to talk to Timothy about exploring the ordination process.

Following the diocesan guidelines, Timothy had me meet with a group of parishioners to help discern my next step. He and the group recommended that I go forward in the ordination process. The night before I met with the larger diocesan ordination commission, I could barely sleep. There were more than a dozen of us "aspirants" going before the commission, and we had heard that only two would be approved. I remember peeking around the corner to see the room where I'd be interviewed. The commission members were already there! One member spied me and said with a laugh, "Come on in – we aren't going to eat you."

The commission – sixteen people in all – sat in a semi-circle and fired questions about everything from my theological views to my personal life. At one point I had a vision of Grandpa Bannister, my mother's father, looking down at me and giving a thumbs-up. It took two weeks for the Bishop's letter to arrive; he said he was admitting me to the ordination process. I did a little dance for joy. He also cautioned that this step, and all future steps in the process, did not guarantee I would be ordained.

To help aspirants continue to discern their calls, the ordination commission assigned them to serve for a year as an intern in a different parish. The priest at my intern parish had a reputation for being uncertain about whether women should be ordained. The first time I walked into his office, I couldn't help noticing the banner from his theologically conservative seminary: it covered an entire wall. Over the course of the year, he was by turns gruff and distant, or cheerful and supportive. I decided to remain as unobtrusive as I could ("wear beige," a friend advised me) and learn as much as possible. One layperson – an elderly lady who attended the Morning Prayer service I led on Sundays – refused to acknowledge me. The rest of the congregation, though, welcomed me.

On Sunday mornings, while I stood thirty feet away at the altar in my cassock and surplice, the kids wriggled and colored pictures in the pew. I keenly missed the feeling of holding them during services and having them crawling over me like kittens.

Already I could see the ordination process came at a cost.

Yet it came with great gifts, too. On Palm Sunday, I read the congregation the words, "Then Jesus cried again with a loud voice, and breathed his last." As I paused for the traditional silence in which the faithful contemplate Jesus' sacrifice, I was struck by a deep and disturbing realization of what it meant for Jesus to die. I was struck by the fact that, even though I sinned over and over, Jesus had loved me so much he died for me. The impact was physical: my heart beat so loudly I wondered if the congregation could hear it. I thought to myself, "I will never, ever again doubt that there is a God – I can feel the living God alive in me. This is *real*."

I started seminary the same day Willy and Adam started kindergarten. Most Episcopalians in the ordination process go to an Episcopal seminary for the three years it takes to get a masters degree in Divinity. But to limit disruption to the kids, I decided, with the Bishop's consent, to spend my first two years at nearby Duke Divinity School and move us all to an Episcopal seminary for only one last year.

When the three kids left on the school bus in the mornings, I'd depart for Duke, then be back in time to greet them at the bus in the afternoons. I'd be Mama till bedtime, playing and reading and baking cookies with them and making dinner and giving them baths and rocking them to sleep. Then I'd hit the books. It was thrilling to be back in a classroom after twenty-one years away, taking notes and writing papers – even though I had a lot more work than I'd remembered from college. Often I'd be up till two or three in the morning, finishing a paper or cramming for a test. The only way I could keep myself awake the next morning in class was by making sure my pen was moving, taking notes. Being both student and mother was almost more than I could handle. And I wondered if my time with Jesus – sensing his presence and his love – was beginning to lose out to the demands of academic life.

For my last year I attended Virginia Theological Seminary in Alexandria, Virginia, mostly because it was closest to our home and we could return easily to see friends. Several seminary families living in our building helped us move into our small, subsidized apartment. Fortunately, Ben could work from our home computer and needed to make only one trip back to his office during the year. But the transition was wobbly for the kids. On the first day of school, one came home and sobbed for more than an hour about being away from friends back home. As I offered words of comfort, I thought angrily, "What have I done to this poor child? God, why are you asking me to sacrifice their sense of security?"

Soon, though, the children made friends and joined soccer and softball teams. And always I'd tell them, "It's only for one year, then we'll be back in Chapel Hill." We had rented out our house, after all. I was certain I'd find a job close to home.

In Virginia, I immersed myself in Anglican liturgy, Anglican thought, Anglican friends. Even though I had enjoyed and learned from the diversity of denominations at Duke, I felt most at home amidst the theological open-mindedness of Episcopalians. My professors predicted I would make a good parish priest. At the time, I never questioned how I could be both a successful parish priest and the involved mother I loved being.

My sense of a call to ministry flourished. I wrote in a paper, "I pray that, in the months and years ahead, God will grant me the power to reach out for Christ's loving grasp, to empty myself of my fears and anxieties, and to perceive clearly my ministry and mission so that, as I do, I may by grace show forth a vision of God's kingdom. While I have yet to learn the actual steps I will take, I do know in whom I am grounded and on whom my gaze is fixed."

In June 1998, after finishing seminary, I was ordained as a transitional deacon, the step before being ordained a priest. Later that afternoon, as our family drove to South Carolina to the family reunion, I wore my clergy collar for the first time in public. I felt a strange sense of separation as people at the Shell station and the Waffle House stared at me. When I arrived at the reunion, my extended family wasted no time reminding me of my new status. My cousins asked me to say the blessing over dinner. One cousin greeted me by making in the air a big sloppy sign of the cross, bowing with hands folded, and calling me "Your reverency." Another cousin greeted me somberly with, "So Liz, how many souls have you saved this year?"

Two months later I moved my books and files into a tiny office at a parish in Durham, North Carolina, only 25 minutes from our house, and began my work as full-time Assistant Rector. The next May, I was ordained a priest in a festive service at the church. Family and friends poured in. Timothy preached a clever, funny sermon that started with "how to make a good hollandaise sauce" and ended with "how to make a good priest." Parishioners offered music on flute, saxophone, organ and drums. A church member quilted me an exquisite stole. My mother was in a wheelchair by then, but I went over to her in the front pew and served her and my father communion. After the service, fellow clergy knelt before me to receive the traditional blessing from "the newest priest in the Church." I celebrated the Eucharist for the first time the next day and felt a stab of love and joy as I consecrated bread and wine as the body and blood of Christ.

Over the next years, I sensed God's presence with me as I celebrated the Eucharist, preached, taught, counseled, supervised Christian formation for all ages and visited newcomers, the sick, and the lonely. I felt God's love as I baptized infants shining with holy water from the font, sat with a woman as her husband of more than forty years surrendered to death, designed education programs to invigorate learning about Church tradition and mission, organized festivals to gather parishioners in celebration, accompanied teens on rope courses and into searching discussions about life. I memorized parts of the Eucharistic liturgy so I could look directly at the congregation for a greater sense of connection. I delivered sermons enthusiastically and learned to write for people's ears, using short sentences that ended with key words. At meetings, I offered a "servant leadership" model of encouraging participation and input from others rather than simply telling people what to do.

I learned to pace myself on Sunday mornings, when I had to stay energized for celebrating or preaching at three services, teaching adult education, being the go-to person for questions and problems in the nursery and Sunday School, and hearing concerns of parishioners as they greeted me before and after the liturgies. Outside the parish, I attended clergy gatherings and community outreach meetings. The bishop asked me to serve on the diocesan Commission on Ministry, the group that only a year before had approved me for ordination, and on a committee that offered pastoral care in situations of clergy sexual misconduct. My work often filled me with joy. Connecting with and serving parishioners, the community and God brought sheer delight.

But I also felt the strain. I had little time left over to reflect and re-charge, little time to care for my family – let alone myself. My engagement calendar was crammed. The work was never done. Many meetings occurred on nights and weekends, times when I also wanted to be with my kids. Like my colleagues, I often had to wrest myself from dinner-table conversation at 6:30 in order to get to a 7 PM church meeting. One of my children begged me to finish writing my sermons by Friday night, "so you can have at least some time on Saturday to play with us." Several times, my back went into debilitating week-long spasms.

I hadn't imagined this kind of life when my seminary professors were predicting my "success" in the parish.

Finally I switched to part-time ministry and went on to other parishes. In the places where I have served, parishioners connected deeply with me and responded with hugs, cards, and joy to the way I led services, preached, and conveyed God's love to them. Supervisors often respected and affirmed my ministry, too, but I sometimes also felt marginalized and that my role as a priest was downplayed. At all times, I continued to try to discern God's path for me.

Meanwhile, I explored ways outside the parish to live out my ordination vows and find work that matched my gifts. I taught pastoral care courses to rural pastors through Duke's Caring Communities program. At Duke Divinity School, I precepted for years in a pastoral-care course and led spiritual formation groups, workshops, and retreats. Just after my father died, and as my mother was in her last years, I wrote about pastoral issues concerning death for the Duke Institute on Care at the End of Life. I earned a certificate in spiritual direction through a two-year training program.

In 2008, after much reflection and with my bishop's blessing, I left parish work. I now focus on leading spiritual formation groups at Duke Divinity, leading workshops and retreats, offering spiritual direction, and serving as a supply priest ("riding circuit" like my great-grandfather). I also do my own writing about topics that have long smoldered inside me. Editing jobs help supplement my income. I think I'm moving closer to who I am and what my gifts are, to "letting my life speak," as the author Parker Palmer would say. My Rehoboth colleagues have provided a safe place to reflect on and tell the truth about my experiences. They also have helped me realize I can fulfill my ordination vows outside the parish.

Still, I struggled with my decision to be non-parochial. At the start of a clergy meeting, the convener asked us each to say our name and parish. As my turn approached, I felt awkward about having to say I had chosen *not* to be on the staff of a parish. I decided to list the types of things I do and add that I've served in three congregations. When I mentioned my discomfort to a priest friend, she reminded me, "If you were in a congregation now, you'd be living a false life. You are living your calling."

I wasn't prepared this year for what happened in Holy Week. For the first time in over a decade, I could decide where I spent the "Triduum," the three holy days starting on Maundy Thursday and ending on Easter Sunday. On Thursday night I found myself sitting awkwardly in a pew, a voice inside my head asking: "What is a priest doing in a pew on Maundy Thursday?" I even considered, in a momentary flash, applying for a congregational position I knew was open. When I got home, I looked up the job description and realized that, honestly, the duties did not fit what I can best offer.

On Good Friday, I went to Duke Chapel, since the service was held mostly in darkness and I knew no one there. The anonymity soothed my turbulence and allowed me to enter into the heartbreak of Jesus' death. At other services that weekend, though, I wondered whether I should be at the altar. I also realized I was too focused on myself during Holy Week, instead of on Jesus' sacrifice, death, and resurrection.

I couldn't help but question if I were fulfilling my ordination vows as a non-parochial priest. Finally on Easter Sunday afternoon, I opened my prayer book to the service for the Ordination of a Priest to check exactly what I had promised to do ten years ago. As I stood before the Bishop, he had told me:

You are called to work as pastor, priest, and teacher ... and to take your share in the councils of the Church. As a priest, it will be your task to proclaim by word and deed the Gospel of Jesus Christ, and to fashion your life in accordance with its precepts. You are to love and serve the people among whom you work, caring alike for young and old, strong and weak, rich and poor. You are to preach, to declare God's forgiveness to penitent sinners, to pronounce God's blessing, to share in the administration of Holy Baptism and in the celebration of the mysteries of Christ's Body and Blood, and to perform the other ministrations entrusted to you. In all that you do, you are to nourish Christ's people from the riches of his grace, and strengthen them to glorify God in this life and in the life to come. My sister, do you believe that you are truly called by God and his Church to this priesthood?

"I believe I am so called," I said.

"Do you ... commit yourself to this trust and responsibility?"

"I do."

Ten Easters later, I scanned the list of priestly duties. I knew I still carried out those tasks. Maybe, I reflected, this was more a question of my own discomfort. How easy is it, after all, to walk an atypical path? Could I find peace with what I see as my actual gifts and limitations, with how I sense I am called to serve? Could I learn to live out the gift of what I feel is my most authentic self?

Sometimes I revisit the question, Is the priesthood truly my vocation? Does it meet Frederick Buechner's standard: "The place God calls you to is the place where your deep gladness, and the world's deep hunger, meet"? Does it square with Parker Palmer's intention, that "the life I am living is the same as the life that wants to live in me"? Does it concur with the character in Gail Godwin's novel *Evensong*, who remarks, "Something's your vocation if it keeps making more of you"? I know that each of these phrases resonates strongly with my experience as a priest. I have felt my ordination stretching me in ways I never would have done on my own. I've had to juggle my vocation as a priest with my vocation as a mother, sometimes fully satisfying neither call. I've encountered overloaded expectations, crises and exhaustion.

But I've also known unimaginable joy as I feel the power of God's love coursing through me and leading me to spread that love to others. I pray that, just as I once perceived the warming winter sunlight on my face, I will continue to sense the movement of God's holy, unpredictable, and astounding Spirit in my life – and be able to discern honestly, and with integrity, where my next steps might lead.

Write About:

—Your first awareness of God

—Your experience with other faiths

—What—if you were on your deathbed now—you would regret not having done in your life. What might you do about this?

—Baptism

—Religious differences within your family

—Injuries and how they change your plans

—An atypical path you have considered, perhaps taken

The Roux

Marilyn Hein

Not long ago, I was standing at the stove with a Louisiana friend watching as she began a shrimp gumbo for a birthday party we were giving. "Start with a roux," she said.

"What is a roux?" I asked.

"A roux", she said, "is flour browned in oil very carefully because it is the foundation for a fine gumbo."

I feel as if my life and faith were started in a finely-prepared roux. I had the best of both worlds—my mother grew up in a large Presbyterian Church in Chicago with an outstanding Christian Education program; my father was raised in a small, rural Methodist church. It was there that he learned to sing. Though not religious fanatics, we could be found at church every time the doors were open and in the South that was often—four different activities on Sunday, choir, Wednesday evening Prayer meeting, and summer camp. Through saying prayers at bed-time and grace at meals, my mother made conversation with God a natural part of living.

Since we went to church every time the doors were open, I sang a dozen hymns a week. And at home my father loved to sing hymns in harmony with my sisters and me. When I became troubled, an obscure phrase would come to me as a word from God.

It was a good thing I was sautéing in a nourishing roux growing up because twice as a preschooler I spent months in the hospital with life threatening illnesses. At two, I swallowed a price tag staple, choked, and the staple slipped down into my lung. It lived hidden in the darkness of my body so long that infection completely took over the lung. I gasped so hard for breath that my good lung collapsed and a medical team performed an emergency tracheotomy in the ambulance on the way to the hospital. I was flown to Children's Hospital in Chicago for two unsuccessful procedures. Finally a surgery removed the foreign object. In 1949, penicillin was ready for humans, making me the youngest child ever to receive this antibiotic for major surgery.

If that wasn't enough for my young mother, I contracted polio at age five. I went to kindergarten the first day and came home with what my parents thought was the flu. After a week in bed I began dragging my right leg when I walked. The first procedure I endured, and by far the most painful in my life, was a spinal tap. Three doctors bent me in half on my side in the bed. With a huge needle they drew the spinal fluid, which to me looked like tomato soup. After the diagnosis I spent two weeks in intensive care, where I was wrapped in hot, damp, wool rug pads twice a day. Then I lived a month in isolation with only a large crib in the room. Period. If I dropped anything on the floor, it was thrown away. Fortunately, as I was on the first floor, my bed could be moved over by the window so I could wave to my parents and sisters. After isolation, I spent six months in a convalescent center learning to walk again. Not only did I practice walking, holding on to parallel rails, I also exercised in the facility pool. Although I was only five, I had been swimming since I was eighteen months old because my mother was a Red Cross swimming instructor. I was the only one out of all the children who loved the pool and spent many hours there walking from side to side.

Once a week my mother would drive over the mountains in California to see me. I hated being there all alone; I was a total extrovert with a vivid imagination. I begged my mother to take me home every time she came and felt devastated every time she left me. It is a wonder we even speak to each other now.

But I just lived through it. I was devoid of any conversation with God or anyone else. I felt totally alone and so full of self-pity. I wanted to heal on my own, at home on our farm. I was taught by word and deed, I am sure, to endure everything and just move on. That worked pretty well until I was a young adult.

Although my childhood was spent in and out of hospitals, I thrived as a youth—I was a leader at church and at school. I sang in the sanctuary choir, served on the Stewardship committee, was an officer in our local presbytery and synod youth organizations. I was president of my class at school and played in the band. I also raised cattle for 4-H, rode horses, and worked in the fields in the summer.

Being raised on a working farm was just as important as my degrees in helping me fulfill my vocation. I learned how to be a self-starter, to work alone, to work hard no matter how hot or tired I was. Even though I'd had polio, my parents were wise enough not to pamper me. I was given the same responsibilities as everyone else on the farm. We all cut the weeds out of the soybeans, picked up hay bales in the fields, helped with the tobacco. We raked magnolia leaves and mowed the grass, picked strawberries and sweet corn. Agrarian life gave me a deep personal strength that I would use and need throughout my life.

My relationship with God became as close as my breath. Every night I spent time reading and reflecting on scripture and praying fervently. My pattern seemed to be that when things were going well, my relationship with God was constant, but when I was in the hospital, away from friends and family, I abandoned God.

Just before my senior year in high school, I began a slow sautéing process of call and vocation. It was a warm Arkansas summer evening at a national Presbyterian youth conference; the tree frog chorus was as raucous as our singing had been at vespers. The preacher sent us off to contemplate, alone. In sixteen-year-old fashion I agonized over what to do with my life. As a child of the sixties, surrounded by the vicious Viet Nam war, I felt compelled to make a difference in the world. I thought seriously about social work—everyone was doing that then. It seemed the only vocation for people like me.

All of a sudden, though, and seemingly out of nowhere, I had an epiphany. I knew what I wanted to do. God called me to the ministry of the church, for there I would work with everyone and persuade them, by word and deed, to work for the world God intended.

Now I had a direction, a purpose; I was happier than I had ever been. I made straight A's my senior year in high school and felt disciplined for the first time. Instead of talking in class and being "too enthusiastic," as my teachers had said all through school, I now worked hard.

The difficulty came when I had to break the news to my mother that I was not going to her alma mater, Maryville College, but to Bethel College, a Cumberland Presbyterian school. She was crushed and, for the only time ever, sent my father in for evening prayers that night. He never prayed with me at night; she did. Daddy knelt beside my bed and begged me to change my mind. Later my mother tried to talk me out of the ministry because—now the family secret comes out—my aunt had a master's degree in Christian Education and had worked a year, only to be sent home for lack of funds. The pastor had been paying my Aunt Esther's salary, which he was able to do for one year, hoping that the congregation would pick up the tab the second year. But unfortunately they were not able to fund her employment.

Despite their objections, I was totally convinced that God called me, so off I went. Here I must add: What remarkable parents I had. They believed that I was going to the wrong school and, even more, I was going to be in a field with no security—very low pay and no appreciation. Still, they paid for my education despite their reservations. Nothing was ever said again. They supported me the whole way.

My last month at home, I marched eagerly downstairs every

morning, walked over to the calendar, and marked off another day. I couldn't wait to get out of there. The day before we were supposed to leave, mother called my bluff and announced that we were leaving in an hour. And I burst into tears. After an eight-hour drive across the state of Tennessee with mom and my sisters, we moved my things into the dorm. I turned around to go to the motel with them and my mother informed me that I would stay in the dorm and begin to make friends. I cried again. I stayed alone in my room all evening and didn't meet anyone until the next day. I really did love my family after all. I am sure Mom was thankful she had majored in psychology when it came to raising me.

Though my first night at college was lonely, within two days I had plenty of friends. I adored the whole experience. Early in my first year I became one of the leaders for the evening student chapel services. I have always loved dorm life, and learning. Mom once commented that she was sure that I would not begin to study until there was absolutely no one else to talk to.

Bethel College, McKenzie, TN, was a rich cauldron for me. I grew and deepened personally, spiritually, and professionally. The dean informed me that women were not pastors and I guess I accepted that news, then at least. Women were Church Educators and moreover churches needed the Educator to be the secretary or the musician as well. There was no choice for me — I neither type nor spell. Fortunately, I had years of musical training in instruments and voice.

As a double major in Music and Christian Education, music was the more demanding. It was a 90-hour degree and no minor was even needed, let alone another major. Not only was music all-consuming, I also fell in love with my voice teacher, which was verboten. I ended up with a broken heart but I still loved music. And I dropped my Christian Education major after flunking a Church History final; you see, we were practicing opera until 2:00 AM every morning. The professor mercifully gave me one afternoon to study and then administered the exam again. I was getting so much satisfaction out of the music that I mistakenly thought my call was changing.

I spent a fifth year in graduate school in music. Music had been exciting, invigorating, and very spiritual in college. But after only one semester at a state university I realized that my love was for the church, its music and its education, not music for music's sake.

Fortunately, I was also directing the youth choir at church and helping with the youth fellowship. Two of the parents of the youth group were trained by the denomination to teach demonstration Church School classes. These two saints took me under their wings and began asking me to help them. They sent me to week-long Church School workshops that touched me deeply and set me on my life-long vocational path of Christian Education. I had a lot to learn and I would run into difficulties, but I was ready to start the journey.

In my forty years God placed me in five different situations. My first call was the hardest. After two years the minister asked the session to terminate my position. At the time I was away in Nashville for a meeting of Church Educators. Upon arriving home I was met with frantic messages to call a friend, who was also a session member, immediately. The story seemed to be that the three-person committee put in place to review the pastor's work came in with a negative report. His reply was that there was no way he could work with me, as I was keeping him from doing his job. This was the early seventies; the pastor and the session except for one were all middle-aged businessmen. The furniture store owner said: "Well if that's the case, let's fire her." The conversation then became about me.

After much deliberation it was decided that another session meeting should be held the next night, when I would be home to attend. I arrived at the meeting—the yard filled with all my friends. The pastor turned the meeting over to the pharmacist, the most respected session member in the congregation. The first words out of his mouth were: "I was a member of a church as a young man that split over the firing of one of its pastors. This church is too important to all of us to let that happen so I want to be clear—we will either keep both or ask for the resignations of both."

The pastor apologized and asked for my forgiveness. I spent the next hour with each session member, listening to them comment on their feelings. I was screaming in my head, "Get me out of here!" But I listened and ended up with unrelenting insomnia. I woke up at three in the morning and never got back to sleep. That following Sunday, my mother and grandmother came to church and I followed my mother home that night. On Monday morning she took me to our family doctor and that afternoon to a counselor. My mother taught me another important lesson—when you get in trouble go see your doctor and then get in therapy. This was my first course in learning about depression.

I was able to stay a third year while I applied to graduate school at the Presbyterian School of Christian Education in Richmond, Virginia—a two-year program ending with a Master of Arts in Christian Education.

My favorite course, Reformed Theology, was taught in the living room of our professor. She had purchased a rug but was unwilling to spend the money to have it bound so we sat around the edges of the rug to keep it from curling and discussed the problem of evil — "Does God cause evil?" "Is God really in charge?" It was this experience that finally put out all the fires of doubt that burned inside me head. I became completely committed to Christian Education, as my vocation and as a specific call from God. This school prepared me academically and experientially for a full career in a local congregation.

A second call took me to San Antonio, Texas, to learn how to administer a large Christian Education program. This church had been a demonstration school for all the teachers in Texas to visit and learn from. My third call kept me still in the South, midway down Florida. I began to soar. I learned how to write curriculum as we designed all-day children's events, weekend youth retreats, and Vacation Church School. It was also in this congregation that the pastor began to let me share in the liturgy.

The fourth call was probably the hardest in terms of not feeling as if I were accomplishing anything at the church. What I did learn, though, was a great deal about conflict management. The educators in the synod and the presbytery sent me all over, doing workshops in teacher training to give me experience. But these workshops ended up giving me the satisfaction that my job was not providing me.

My parents were certainly right about all three of their objections to my career choice—a non-ordained, even though professional, Educator can be fired by the church one day and gone the next. My salary was so low that I didn't have a savings account for ten years. After my grandmother died, my mother gave me $2,000.00 of the inheritance. My father said to me one time, "Why don't you take, for once, the job that offers you the most money."

But I didn't really care much about money. I made it a practice never to spend that inheritance. It was my cushion. And I was not a shopper. When I was growing up outside Loudon, Tennessee, there were no stores in which to browse and learn to want things. We also didn't watch much television and so weren't influenced by commercials. We were never given much cash to spend. Mom always said that we were rich but all our money was in land and cattle.

I remember once discovering that the church in San Antonio paid more for the decal-edged bulletins than it did for me. I lived as frugally as I had been raised and that was okay with me. The problem came when I couldn't drive cars and live in apartments up to the standards of my congregation. I was humiliated one Easter when the pastor told me that an anonymous gift had been given for me to go buy a nice dress for Easter.

Rewards in this profession come from self-satisfaction and from the trust children and youth placed in me. There is little institutional appreciation. But here is the good news and what my parents missed. I didn't need any of the three things they told me I wouldn't get. I didn't need security, money or appreciation. I was doing work I loved that fully satisfied me. I was respected by my colleagues in ministry. What else did I need?

God surprised me while I was working in Augusta. A friend stopped by for the night on the way to begin seminary. She had found a program in San Francisco that would take our degree in Christian Education and let us go one more year, or two summers, and graduate with the Master of Divinity, the degree required for ministers. She left at six a.m. and later that morning I walked a postcard down to the post office inquiring about that program. I enrolled and graduated. Having gone to all southern schools, I found San Francisco a mind-expanding adventure. Finally a life-long dream of mine was coming true.

As the time approached for my ordination service, my sister reminded me that women were not supposed to be ministers. I had felt for a long time that I was on the outside of my family looking in. Now I was doing one more thing that would separate us. The distance I felt was caused by several factors—I was away for long periods of time as a young child; there is often discomfort between the care giver and the one cared for; my college was a long way from home; my calls were several states away except for one; working in churches kept me away from home on high holy days.

But to my great surprise, when I was ordained at the age of fifty, my mother sat on the front pew weeping because my father was no longer here. My sister participated in the ordination, dressing me in the robe they gave. Mother was so proud of me that she put flowers in the sanctuary at Christmas and Easter in my honor for several years after that. The greatest symbol I have of the confidence my family placed in me was when my mother asked me to perform her second marriage.

Because of my diverse experiences throughout the first twenty years of my ministry, I was fully prepared for my fifth call. I became a regional governing body educator in eastern North Carolina. I was able to answer people's questions without hesitation; I could support committees, encouraging others to grow in their faith and skills. I was able to preach more than I had time for. I felt completely prepared for this call and love my work and profession.

God blessed me again right after my ordination with a trip to Taizé, a protestant monastery in the south of France. We sang three services a day, meditated during those services. We had Bible study and an hour of meditation after that. Without my even asking God to take away all the resentment and hurts in my life, after seven days of being fully absorbed in the contemplative life, my anger and disappointments were gone. Conversation and hymns were an integral part of my spiritual life and, over half way through my life I learned about silence and listening.

Now I am entering a new phase of my life—preparing for retirement. Because of the economy, and controversies, churches have less and less money. I have continued to live a frugal lifestyle even though I now make a living wage, so I have been able to save the total amount allowed by law.

When my job does come to an end, I will have to decide if I should see what comes or if I should make plans. I have an interest in retooling churches for the future—encouraging congregations to reach out to young adults, supporting educators, encouraging young ministers. A call is formed in the midst of God's people; it does not happen in a vacuum. So I will wait and see what God has in store for me.

I was raised in a slow-cooked roux, sautéed for years, and

became a gumbo that has nourished and fulfilled me and, I trust, those whom I have served.

Write About:

—How your childhood prepared you for life in the church

—Childhood health issues

—Childhood epiphanies

—"Women's work"

—Music in faith

—Money and your congregation

—Each congregation you have served

—Your future

More Than Skin Deep

Marcia Mount Shoop

The "history" (read herstory) of my calling has some layers to it. There's the epidermis. The family lineage: fourth generation ordained, Presbyterian heritage with skills passed down. There's an obviousness about this layer of my call that makes it seem pat to people. They don't know what a journey it is, how many ways God has patiently coaxed me to see who I am in the complexity of family, experience, and what the world and I need from each other. My family history is a part of the story, but there's so much more that God has done and is doing that runs much deeper than the epidermis.

Underneath, my call started where we all do, in that subterranean place, where the cells of ocean and wind and flesh find concreteness and make each of us. Grief and hope decorated the womb where I gestated. My mother miscarried a baby right before I was conceived, and my oldest sister, Allison, died a few years before I was born. The two living sisters who greeted me into the world were fair-skinned and red-headed; I was darker with brown hair—the most like Allison, my mom has always said.

I anticipate grief; more than that I feel it deeply for people. But it's not just grief that I feel; feeling itself is something I have always done with pronounced intensity. I think it's pretty fitting that I was born while my mother was blessing out the doctor because the drugs weren't working and she was feeling it all. Feeling things and expecting, yearning for others to feel them, too. That's kind of who I've always been. But that kind of intensity is not always what people want or need from me, so I've had to learn to be artful about how much I expose and extend my nerve endings. But the call started then—to be

44

present and to feel and to invite others to come closer to God's mysterious power and presence.

I grow into my call still—everyone does. I resist. I embrace my own interpretation. I try to make it something that it isn't. God keeps gently offering unlikely moments of clarity.

I got a Bible in fourth grade with my name in gold in the front, "Marcia Whitney Mount." With it I held a pearl of great price. I still take that Bible wherever I travel and it sits by my bed otherwise. In eighth grade I read it from cover to cover—my own *lectio divina*, punctuated sometimes by theological musings I would write on scraps of paper. It was my nightly discipline and it poured into me with nuance and sentient understanding like water right from a spring, sediment and all.

Church has been a given. Growing up I would go even on the rare Sunday when the rest of my family hibernated and took a Sunday off. In middle school we lived close enough so I could walk. I felt restless until I got there and found my place to sit down. I belonged there in God's house regardless of how cold or warm the reception was from the saints who were gathered that Sunday. Being good Presbyterians, we felt no need for effusive welcome or attention. The epidermal, obvious, narrative is that I've been a devoted church goer all of my life. The subterranean, more-difficult-to-parse narrative is that it has been a complicated relationship.

When I was fifteen I was raped by the boy I was "dating." We'd been to the movies a few times and he had been pushing for more, sitting near me in Latin class. The rape and the abuse and the stalking afterward are things that I ran from, but have had to return to repeatedly. Trauma does that and I am no exception, though I tried for years to be one. My calling splintered because I thought I wasn't perfect anymore. I resolved to keep things in order (and as subterranean as possible) the best way I knew how. Church, the Bible, my family: these have all been simultaneous mainstays and landmines.

After the rape, I remember Jesus holding me in the dark. Jesus knew the whole story and understood and loved me. Jesus was home and hope. But, back then I didn't run into this same Jesus at church, except on a few rare occasions that seemed like strange exceptions to some mainline Protestant rule about emotions and feeling. At church the Jesus I met again and again was about justice and service and forgiveness for all the rotten things I had done—but forgiveness for my impurity, because of what had happened, felt like strange food that I just could not bring myself to swallow. Church was a place where I needed to convince everyone that I had it together—I could never be honest about the shards of myself that were scattered in the shadows of my life. But Jesus stayed close and gently whispered the truth to me over and over again.

My knees buckled the first time I felt *that* Jesus really show up full on at church. I was twenty-six years old. Seigle Avenue Presbyterian Church in Charlotte, North Carolina, is where the Jesus who held me in the dark came out into the light, in the lives of my brothers and sisters in Christ. It was the music there that let me feel that truth. "I'm Coming up on the Rough Side of the Mountain" overtook me. Ms. Clara sang strong even though she only had one lung; Wilma had a quiet sure spirit that kept her strong for her kids. They sang it together. "Oh Lord I'm striving, trying to make it through this barren land." My body's brokenness was okay there. I must have cried a river in the months that followed. Integrity felt good. God's call seeped in.

Mingled in these startling Jesus-encounters, I have always been drawn to study, learn, and achieve. I love studying religion and thrived in that work as a student. Divinity school was both epidermal and subterranean, as was my PhD work. I found companions on my journey—not just colleagues but theologians like Origen, Cyril, and Alfred North Whitehead. I found poets and feminists and philosophers and sages of all stripes— Buddhist, Tewa, Cherokee, Jewish, Muslim, Vedic, Monophysite.

I also found a mentor, a sister who walked parallel and criss-crossing paths to mine, in my professor Wendy Farley at Emory University. She understood me as a theologian and she showed me myself in that light. With her help my writing and thinking began to feel free to line up with my feeling. God's call still works to find its way into this work and urges me to integrate my experiences and my work.

Woven into the timeline of study and church are a wedding, three pregnancies, two births, geographical changes, and churches calling me to serve. My ordination in the Chicago Presbytery encapsulates so much complexity and blessing. This church that turned out to be my first call was a church that I couldn't stomach when we first moved to Chicago. We had moved for my husband John's work as an NFL football coach. I'd had to leave Seigle Avenue—a multiracial church living the Gospel in a government housing project in Charlotte, NC, and a healing ministry on every level. Trying to find a church home after that felt like trying on shoes that didn't fit. Some truly hurt—the constriction was unbearable for me. Others I just sloshed around in like there was no there, there. Still others I may have really liked at another time in my life, but they just didn't match who I was anymore.

First Presbyterian Church of Libertyville was a large, suburban, affluent, almost entirely homogeneous (read Caucasian, professional, heterosexual) congregation. It also had a reputation for being one of the more conservative churches in the presbytery. On paper it did not seem like a good fit for me. Their minister had been removed and three hundred people left with him to form an Evangelical Presbyterian congregation near by. On paper, the church was troubled, affluent, theologically conservative, and not looking to diversify. I could not have pointed to a demographic I felt less called to for ministry.

But the congregation was much more complicated than all of that. They were earnest, broken, loving, faithful, and open to

God's unlikely creativity. The interview process was an intense unfolding. I wasn't sure what was happening or why, but in between being asked about my views on the inerrancy of scripture and praying for guidance, I began to hear it loud and clear: if they give me a chance, I can be their pastor.

There are many moments of clarity in that place. My ordination, with my dad preaching and Ms. Anne Bradley from Seigle Avenue taking her first plane ride to come to Chicago to sing "On Time God" with the Libertyville choir, is one of them. I still live on that day and all that settled into all of us who gathered there. That church helped teach me who I am—a pastor, a preacher, a theologian, and someone who could minister to people across political and theological boundaries. And, I found out, I am somebody who wants to minister in those contradictions. God stretched me there to recognize all the "otherness" that conceals itself in churches where the spaces for difference are constricted. I learned about inclusion on a deep level in that church and it cultivated in me a new kind of intuition about differences—no matter their character. I believe church should be a place where racial diversity, theological differences, economic disparities, and all that estranges us from each other should find a home.

But the work was intense and I had a little baby boy and a husband who worked seven days a week, often eighteen hours a day. I wasn't good at asking for help. I tried to be available, present, prepared, and responsible; this meant going non-stop until I picked my son up (almost always late) and writing sermons at 2:00 am. It meant dropping things to listen and then living with the stress of not having enough time to get every-thing done. It meant skipping lunch and eating on the run.

Becoming completely helpless when I got pregnant with my daughter was an excruciating reversal for me. I had to let the church take care of me and this reorientation deeply disturbed me. For all of my independence and energy, I now had only a paralyzing nausea and a sense of vocational failure. But the subterranean work of making a new life didn't just form my daughter; it re-formed me and the church. The church took care of my son; they cleaned my house, and they held my hand in silence because I often couldn't move or talk much. They prayed for me and prayed with me. They saw me in my time of trial and they loved me and nourished me even when I couldn't keep anything down.

Before I got pregnant, I can remember driving up to the church some days and saying, "Wow. I get paid for this!" The work felt like a great gift. The truth is I can also remember driving home from work, feeling caught in a huge snowball that was just getting bigger and bigger and moving faster and faster downhill and wanting to find a way out. It was a mix of love and stress, anxiety and affection, competence and helplessness.

Being a good pastor means being lonely sometimes. But having to accept the care and compassion of my church has helped me to be wiser about how to live within that loneliness and not be destroyed by it. Receiving help and being vulnerable to care is an important even if delicate part of being a pastor. It's not just that pastors are human just like everyone else. Giving and receiving is part of the vow we take to proclaim the Good News. No one is just the helper, and no one is just the receiver. We are all both—constantly in need of grace and constantly called to be present to those in need. Jesus invites us into a sacred trust that means we can be at once strong and vulnerable, prophetic and broken.

After all the wonderful care I got from First Presbyterian Church of Libertyville, I had to move just a few weeks before my daughter was born—another job change because of the vagaries of NFL football. Anyone who says football is just a game hasn't walked in my shoes. God's work in my life is tangled up with things like crappy general managers, injured quarterbacks, interceptions, missed field goals, and fickle owners. I commuted seven hours one-way to finish my masters. I commuted four hours one-way to get my PhD. Perhaps the most telling measure of how much we've moved is that my daughter gestated in Chicago, was born in Tampa, FL, turned one in Oakland, California and turned three in Chapel Hill, North Carolina. Four cities in three years—two churches with calls and two stints as theologian-in-residence. Sometimes I feel like I've been piecing this thing together, but then I see providential thread that has refused to let anything fray.

I have rejoiced in each new place and opportunity, and I have grieved having to say goodbye so many times. Preaching and teaching and pastoring in so many places taught me a lot in a very short time. I've grown up fast as a pastor. In the midst of all these transitions, the struggle of family, work, belief, and calling haven't gotten any easier. Working part-time or full-time, with a large staff or a small staff, with days on and days off—no combination exists that allows for a consistently life-giving experience. Yearning to serve and yearning to mother and not having the hours in the day or the reserves to do it all; struggling to assert and to find my voice and to know how to receive and ask for help; just slowing down and really breathing like I am supposed to—all of it can feel insurmountable sometimes. I can get frustrated with how days rush themselves when I want them to meander. The rushing doesn't just get under my skin, but it gets into my habits, my muscles and it seems to be the only thing I know how to do. At the same time I can be restless about stasis and triviality. I love being in the thick of things and feeling how a community finds its way in God's vision.

But sometimes I wonder about all the other things I feel—like irritation, fatigue, and inadequacy. Where do those things fit in? I feel anger sometimes toward my husband for not helping at home more and even toward my kids because they need so much. They are beautiful, complicated children and I hate getting angry with them. I get frustrated with not being able to finish sentences or thoughts and then in turn with not being able to really focus on my children because I have so much to do. I can also get frustrated with the Church—with stasis and fear, with homogeneity and lots of other things that get us stuck. At the same time I love all the beautiful saints who make up the church and I am thankful to see who they are and who they can be.

Sometimes this life-work feels like being torn in two, no maybe into a hundred pieces. Being in ministry seems to make these fragments more clear. What other vocation wads all this stuff up in a snarl of responsibility and hope and humanity and says: it's all God's doing? But no neat and tidy theory about "everything happens for a reason" works when you are a minister. I like how Alfred North Whitehead puts it: God is the poet of the world.

God's calling has been more blessed and more intricate than I could have ever dreamed. Sometimes I am overcome with gratitude. The surface and deep tissue of call is iconographic to be sure. It is like an image of something sacred—always reflecting and refracting meaning, but also always retaining some of its mystery and unspeakability. My call is beautiful and wonderful and burdensome and hard. My call is colorful and intricate and incomplete.

Right now I am learning and relearning some good pastoral habits—not those that are second nature to me, like listening or being present to those in crisis or being able to lead groups and preach good sermons. Right now I am learning how to be at home in my life and in my call with more integration, more integrity. God's generous Spirit is cultivating and expanding what and where my call is.

In everything I do, God calls me to be present, to feel and to invite others to come closer to God's mysterious power and presence. Sometimes I miss being on whatever radar screen you are on when you pastor a church. Life can get tedious when emptying and filling the dishwasher takes up a lot of your day. My call isn't on sabbatical though. I know that my call to Ministry of Word and Sacrament runs down through my bones—and I feel it there with great assurance and hopefulness. I am becoming more comfortable in my own skin—all the layers of it.

I find sweet symmetry in the way "Rehoboth" has entered my consciousness of late. This Rehoboth, Isaac's third well in Genesis, is all about having room to flourish. It is about open space and provision. I am not sure I was aware of this word before we moved to Chapel Hill and now it surfaces all over the place. God's poetic skill is breathtaking sometimes. It is a blessing to feel provided for, to feel room around you to be who God made you to be. Rehoboth is about abundance, not scarcity. There is enough, plenty in fact. And so I drink from this deep well of God's hopes for me. It feels good to let it seep in and water the spirit of call in my life. I am entangled with kids and what they see and feel and need. I am writing, preaching, teaching, and being quiet when I can. And, I spend some of my time wandering through meadows of green weeds and grass on a beautiful mare who is just getting her bearings in a new herd.

Thanks be to God.

Write About:

—What is skin deep and what is subterranean in your church life?

—Deep feelings

—Your favorite bible

—Receiving care from a congregation

—What has made you feel broken and estranged and imperfect?

—God as the poet of the world

—Different images of Jesus—the public and the private

Questioning Believer: A Journey Into Faith

Nancy Rozak

Religion seemed important in my family, even though my parents never went to church. From a young age, my brothers and I were expected to attend Sunday school and the service afterwards. My mother stayed at home to take care of my two toddler brothers; my dad was usually on the golf course.

Imagine two unaccompanied children boarding a city bus every Sunday morning. I was five and my brother eight. We sat wedged together, as close to the driver as we could get. The ride into town took about twenty minutes. Just inside the city limits the driver stopped the bus and beckoned my brother and me to get off. We stood on the sidewalk and watched the bus pull away from the curb. Across the street was the church. We always managed to find our way.

I remember the long climb up the drab steel and concrete staircase to get to the Sunday school classrooms. A Sunday school teacher who lived in our town drove us home after the morning worship service.

When I was eight, my family moved to a new town where my parents chose to take us to a church close to our new home. Every Sunday morning my dad would load my three brothers and me into the car and drive us to the Community Church to attend Sunday school, followed by the worship service. Congregants referred to us as "drop-offs." Sunday school was a welcoming experience but, during the worship service, I felt uncomfortable being at church without my parents. Some Sundays I fantasized that we were actually four orphaned children. I loved my grandmother's visits because she came to church with us. What a comfort it was having her sitting next to me in the pew. I think I was nine or ten before I began to understand why my parents did not join us. My dad, a Catholic, did not want to leave his church and my mother claimed that she pursued her faith at home, whatever that meant.

I cultivated a powerful prayer life. My prayers were simple and direct, and I rarely went to sleep without offering at least one. I had a fear of the dark so often I would ask God to keep me safe and not let me die. My trust in God must have been somewhat iffy—some mornings I awakened to find myself cowering under my bed with my pillow.

I journeyed through Sunday school filled with unanswered questions like, Who made God so that God could make the world? Or, What existed before creation? Or, How can we know that God is real? Teachers either dismissed my concerns or asked me to stop asking "Silly questions."

Confirmation class, however, helped my faith development. We learned what it meant to be a Christian. We visited other religious congregations and compared them with our non-denominational faith. I found the comparisons fascinating. At my sixth grade confirmation I stood before the congregation and declared my faith in Jesus Christ, feeling filled with an emotional sense that God was with me and within me.

The rituals of the church service continued to pull me in and give me a temporary feeling of wellbeing. I say temporary because, being a strong-willed and stubborn child, I sought to be in control of my life, rather than to consider any sort of plan that God might have had for me. A famous quote in my childhood household was, "Love many and trust few and learn to paddle your own canoe." I just kept paddling. I look back now and realize that God was calling me into relationship, but I was not listening.

At fourteen, I found myself in a girls' boarding school, three hours away from home. My sense of personal control quickly evaporated. The school gave me a rigorous academic schedule, a pair of Buster Brown shoes, and a plain gingham uniform.

Meals were served at strictly appointed hours and lights were to be out at 10 PM. After "lights out" talking was forbidden. I felt homesick for my brothers, my parents, my dog, and, of course, my friends.

If ever I needed God, this was clearly the time. So I prayed, a lot. I also discovered a small monastic chapel within the larger school chapel. It was a small space, defined by floor-to- ceiling cutouts with wooden panels that resembled arched windows. A small altar stood at the front of the space, graced by a lace altar cloth, two brass candlesticks, and a simple cross. This was the place I chose to go when I needed to disappear. This was my refuge.

In the quiet and isolation of the little chapel, God and I became friends. Sitting motionless in one of the plain, unadorned, wooden chairs, I could be alone and silent. No one judged me, pretended to be a friend, or told me where to be and when to be there. I was free to think, to talk to God, and to hide from a life and routine I did not like. I would leave my private sanctuary rested and ready to return to the regimentation.

Chapel attendance was mandatory at this school and religion a required course. Preachers came from nearby churches to conduct Sunday afternoon chapel service. For me, these services were often inspirational and I looked forward to them. Sitting in the pew, I remembered the camaraderie of going to church with my brothers, and I could almost sense the presence of God. I recall leaving chapel, on occasion, feeling inwardly transformed.

Religion class was another matter. I prided myself on asking challenging questions of the instructor. I wanted to know how a big fish could swallow a man or how a sea could part and come back together. I asked: "How was God created?" And, "Might there be a force greater than God?" The teacher invariably responded, "That's just the way it is." What kind of an answer is that, I wondered? I craved classroom discussion about these topics and others, but remained frustrated and discouraged. I weathered the three years – I had no choice – and was relieved to escape the class upon graduation.

In an all girls' junior college, I discovered greater freedom. I did not go to church regularly but I did look forward to worshiping during specific Christian holidays. You might say that I was a CE person (Christmas and Easter). Reflecting back, I believe I was not ready to fully trust God. What if God let me down as so many people had? Where would I turn then? I could not risk losing, and clung to, my private faith.

My prayer life remained a constant. I even found myself praying during the day, at times, with my eyes opened to better appreciate the wonder of God's natural order. The vision of seasonal changes still captures my attention. The magnificent colors in fall, the beauty of snow falling in the quiet of the moonlit night, spring flowers emerging from a once frozen ground, will ever speak to me of a well-conceived plan.

Approaching my junior year in college, I felt ready to take on a big university and all that it might offer. I transferred to the University of Wisconsin where there were few restrictions. Choosing your own path was rarely opposed. I was able to decide which courses to take, times and days I preferred to go to class, and when to go to bed at night. This might sound liberating, but I was not used to being the initiator of my destiny. I was stunned to discover that most instructors were indifferent about class attendance. I was viewed as one among many in class—just a number, not a person. Survival became my initial goal as I struggled to find my way. Unlike boarding school, I did not need to find a place to hide at Wisconsin. I could easily get lost in the crowd. I needed a way to be seen.

These years were a turning point in my life. I began to take control of my own life and felt empowered by my growing sense of accomplishment. I graduated on time, which to me seemed little short of a miracle. Only occasionally did I see the inside of a church in those two years, when I joined a friend of my mother's at her Lutheran service. Again, I depended on my prayer life to keep me connected to God, but I felt that our relationship lacked depth. Still, God remained important to me and I hoped God understood my need to discover who I was supposed to become. Being involved in formal religion took time and my life was just too busy to go to church. Finally I was free to make my own choices and I chose to ignore Sunday worship services altogether.

In 1966 I fell in love and married in 1967. The pastor who married us provided the spark I needed to jumpstart my faith journey. During our premarital counseling sessions, Dr. Reamon spoke of unconditional love, respect, truth and honesty with oneself and others. He brought God's love and God's promise to our wedding ceremony. I was overcome with a sense of God's presence and called my experience a religious transfusion. As we left for our honeymoon a feeling of exhilaration awakened me to the need to get back to church.

Unfortunately, a career in personnel, learning to be a wife, and venturing out into the city of Chicago, took immediate precedence over a deeper relationship with God or to finding a church home. It amazes me how fickle I was. One minute I was fired-up to explore and grow in faith and the next I felt distracted by worldly needs. I continued to let life's busyness keep me from worshiping God in a church community.

The arrival of children in our lives brought me full circle. For me it was important to introduce our children to formal church and I had no intention of dropping my children off at church as I had been. I joined the Presbyterian Church in my town and agreed to teach Sunday school to ensure my involvement. The Director of Christian Education at the church gently guided me toward my call to ministry. She encouraged me to attend workshops on Christian education. She offered me interesting books and articles to read. I loved teaching Sunday school, loved engaging in the discussions I felt I had been denied as a child.

Soon I began to say yes to other opportunities that called me to get more involved in church life. Along with teaching, I became an elder, a deacon, a Bible student, and eventually the chair of the Christian Education committee. My faith life, vastly expanded, was beginning to show fruit-bearing signs. During Sunday worship services, I often imagined a career in service to the church. My thoughts were absorbing and inviting: was God calling me? I had a strong feeling that it was so, but the timing felt wrong.

Raising a family, teaching pre-school, enjoying time as a homemaker, volunteering at church and elsewhere, kept me extremely busy. After all, those were the roles a woman of my generation was expected to play, right? My response to the notion of a call to the ministry was, "Not now God, other roles are expected of me at the moment."

How bold of me! God, fortunately, continued to be as patient with me as he was with Moses, Jeremiah, and the apostles. I continued to convince myself that I could not possibly spend the time required to go into the ministry.

Time passed quickly, so it seemed, and soon my children were in college. My husband was fully absorbed in his career, and I was teaching pre-school part-time while working on my master's degree in Education. I decided that education would allow me to grow professionally but not take up as much time as church ministry. At this point in my life I was ready for a challenge and I knew that education was now a passionate interest. But church life continued to lure me.

Upon graduation I was offered the opportunity to teach several classes in Early Childhood Education at a large community college in my area. The head of my department, a fellow Christian, became a life-long friend and mentor. Content and affirmed in my career as a teacher at the college level, I felt God call me one more time. In 1996 I was approached by a small community church and asked to consider a position as their first

Director of Christian Education. They wanted me to design an educational program that would grow and enrich their Sunday school program. This bright light was just too clear to ignore. I was excited and eager to accept the challenge. In some ways I felt like I was coming home. Here was another call to serve in church ministry and the timing was ideal. I answered the call and big things began to happen.

As the educator in a church of 200 members, I was able to use my background to write curriculum and programming. Setting up the Sunday school program came easily to me and was rewarding. I quickly discovered the heart of my call. I loved to connect with the people. It was an honor and privilege to listen to their joys and concerns, and to walk beside them in their life challenges. Words seem inadequate to convey what it means to be given such trust by others. I felt comfortable, even successful, in the church environment. As I look back I realize that I was just beginning. This was not the full story that God had in mind for me.

I was asked to fill in for the pastor while he was on a summer vacation. This included preaching one Sunday. I agreed as long as the congregation realized that I was far from an ordained minister. I delved into the Bible and worked hours to develop a meaningful message. I survived the Sunday worship experience and was most graciously received and accepted for my efforts.

Soon, I began to yearn for greater biblical and spiritual growth. I felt supported and secure in this church. I was able to teach, minister, write, and even preach. Despite extreme nervousness, I opened myself up to try it all. A big question remained in my mind though. Was I actually responding to God's call or was this just a fulfilling personal experience?

In 1995 I attended a national Presbyterian educator's conference in San Diego. The conference offered workshops, inspiring speakers, and networking opportunities. I was introduced to a program designed for Christian educators seeking to explore their call. If nothing else, I thought, this program just might answer some of my questions relating to the future direction for my life. Upon returning from San Diego, I applied for the Presbyterian Certification process and was accepted into the program. Officially and publicly I entered the academic world of Christian ministry.

Like many life journeys, there are frequently interruptions. In 1998 my husband lost his job as a result of a corporate buy out. After over thirty-five years in his given position, he found himself in a precarious situation. He was too old to make a lateral executive move. Further, he was despondent, shocked, and not at all excited about moving backwards to a lesser position. We weathered the months of unemployment, supported by his severance package; we both knew we needed to find an acceptable answer for our situation. I continued to teach early childhood education at the community college and to remain on the staff at church. Then one early morning, the Holy Spirit sent me a jolt that I could neither miss nor ignore.

Have you ever asked God for guidance and specifically stated, "Please, God. Make it clear?" I frequently speak to God in this manner and God often responds. Well, God spoke to me on that day and the message was unmistakable: it is time to move on! After thirty-three years living in the same town, I was hearing, "Time to move on."

It took me a few weeks to internalize this message. Questions flashed across my controlling mind. "Do you mean, God, that we should leave all of our friends? Are you suggesting that we uproot our home of 30 years? How will my husband feel, our children, our friends? And where will we go, not to mention what will we do?"

God and I were in regular dialogue.

After several candid discussions, my husband admitted that it was indeed time to move on. We were ready to make a new beginning. As the proactive player of our relationship, I realized that I would be expected to initiate the change. I wanted to continue in Christian ministry and to work toward my certification. The sense of call to ministry was growing stronger and so was my willingness to respond. Our original, long-term plan was to someday retire in North Carolina. Because of its diverse cultural and academic environment, the area called the Triangle was our first choice. A search of the internet, initially, produced no available positions for a Christian educator. Once again, I considered pushing away my call to ministry. I was somewhat accustomed to forfeiting dreams and I could do it again.

Into the closet of failed dreams I cast my intentions of becoming a Certified Educator in the Presbyterian Church. I thought to myself, "So what"? I can go back to early childhood education. I am quite sure I can find something in that field. Indeed, there are more career options in early childhood than in Christian education.

I sent out resumes to jobs in early childhood education, expecting that I would most likely receive one or two interviews. During the waiting period I continued to work on my course materials to become a Certified Christian Educator. I enjoyed the readings and writing required for certification. The experience was thought provoking, reassuring, and empowering. I found myself wrestling with theology and spirituality. It was now up to me to use my acquired Bible skills to discover the meaning of Bible Scripture. It was my challenge to interpret questions like: Why was Jonah was swallowed by a big fish? and What caused the Red Sea to part for Moses?

It was during one of my study sessions that I finally woke up. "Stop lying to yourself for once," I said. "Follow the call you are feeling! You do not want to return to early childhood; you feel a strong pull to Christian education and you need to respond."

I finished my studies for the night and went to the computer to check again, the Presbyterian website. There it was! I was staring, in disbelief, at an opening for a Christian educator, in

Durham, North Carolina, in the heart of the Triangle. I navigated to the website of Westminster Presbyterian Church. With each click of the mouse, with each window I opened, I knew that this was just what I dared to dream about. I sent off my resume. Two months later, Westminster called me to serve as their Director of Christian Education. I had found my home.

Perhaps this experience will remain the life-changing highlight of my journey. My eyes were opened to Christian education, meaningful worship, Christian community, and the best chance ever to be mentored and nurtured. Within two years of my arrival, I received my Certified Educators degree. My journey at Westminster continued to roll along and I would pinch myself, on occasion, to be sure that I was not living a dream. My husband and I began to put down roots in our new community.

At Westminster I lead classes, create programs, minister to children, youth and adults, and guide an energetic team of volunteers. I enjoy being a Stephen Minister and networking with other educators and ministers in my Presbytery. New Hope Presbytery is welcoming and encourages me to stay involved. In this place and time I can minister to others and find support for myself.

In 2004, I was asked to join a group called Rehoboth, an ecumenical group of female ministers who meet once a month. One of our sessions was led by Carol Henderson, an author and writing coach. Carol captivated us as she shared her experience of writing a book and following it to publication. She guided us through prompts to do some writing ourselves. It was an inspiring program. Processing her session while driving home, I once again was jolted into a new reality. Hidden from my conscious mind, locked away as if in a tower room, lay a desire to write.

Through a Rehoboth grant, I was able to work with Carol privately for a four-month period. She guided me to a greater level of fulfillment in relationship to my own writing. I no longer feel blocked about my writing; I am content to put pen to paper and express my deepest thoughts. I intend to take advantage of other course opportunities in creative writing to stay connected.

Today I enjoy my position at Westminster. After a decade my call remains purposeful and vibrant. God has led me with perseverance and patience. For that I give thanks. It is my belief that God calls each of us to lead a life of fulfillment. For me, this includes a church community and the support of other faithful believers.

My journey is far from over but I know now that I am not an orphan. I belong to God's family. God is my parent. I depend on God to live in me, guide me, and send me into each day armed with faith and courage. I hold dreams for my future as I journey, looking to hear and respond to God's call in my life. I will continue to question and to wonder. And God, I trust, will continue to remain persistent and yet patient in my life.

Write About:

— Feeling abandoned

— The history of your prayer life

— Your parents' relationship to church

— Raising children in the church

— Time to move on

— "Stop lying to yourself"

— God as a parent

Long Black Robes

Caroline Craig Proctor

I became a high priestess of a 2,000-year-old religion—kicking and screaming all the way. Even now, when I remove the colorful Guatemalan stole I wear over my shoulders, unzip the black robe and all the stories it holds, I wonder: how did I come to be here? How did this become my uniform, my costume? Was it genetics? Privilege? The years I spent growing up in church tapping the back of the pew in front of me? Was it a direct path? A calling? My answers differ, depending on the day.

One day I would point to a seven-year-old girl who walked out of church in her white patent leather shoes and greeted the man in the black robe, her father's best friend. He asked her, "What do you want to be when you grow up?"

"A fireman," she said, which seemed like a brave and important thing to be. She wanted to rescue people in burning buildings and cats stuck in trees.

"You could be a minister when you grow up," he told her," if you want to be."

The little girl considered this idea. But at that point she had never seen a minister who seemed happy in black robes. Still, ministers were rather important and able to capture the attention of grownups. Looking back, she realized that was probably the week the Presbyterian Church in the South ordained the first woman to the office of Minister of Word and Sacrament. So there's one version of the story about me and the black robes.

Another day I would point to a young woman in college who wanted very much to have her life mean something, to matter in some significant way. She refused to take religion courses, even though they were the most interesting to her. because the only thing she could imagine with a religion major was a career in "the church" and she did not want that. She was an adequate student but most loved working outside of school: organizing shoveling brigades to clear snow from the elderly town folks' driveways, beginning a recycling program, and attending visiting lecturers' talks. It was relationships that enticed her more than articles of faith, the ground beneath her feet more than the promise of something better later.

She had a mentor, David Kaylor, who still lives fully and spreads joy. He invested his free time with friends on tennis courts, and with neighbors under Habitat for Humanity house roof trusses, and with companions at protests on behalf of the people in South Africa and Nicaragua. He fed a family of seven out of his large back yard garden. In retirement he busies himself in his woodworking shop turning bowls out of tree stumps, playing with grandchildren, and keeping up with current theology. He laughs a lot and doesn't too often sport a black minister's robe, but when he does he preaches from the prophets. He does all these things, he says, because of Jesus.

Dr. David Kaylor first introduced me to a radical Jesus who was outrageous and uncontainable and righteous and interesting. He first challenged me to an act of justice I was too afraid to commit, and I remember this often with humility and regret and gratitude because it drove me to seminary. Here is what happened.

Spring break of my senior year I joined a study trip to Central America led by David and a political science professor, Dr. Brian Shaw. We went to Guatemala in the midst of their civil war. The dramatic beauty of the landscape took my breath away. The gentle humility of the people gave it back to me. I trembled before the terror carved into their wide-eyed faces as they dared to tell us of the bloodletting that soaked the mountains around us. I felt the weight of the dirt floor beneath me, wishing to sink into it, as Betsy Alexander, a graduate of the college I attended, spoke of teaching nutrition and literacy—and of the bodies of her students dumped near her stoop. She cried again telling us. This was a path someone like me could take, I thought, but I did not want it. Maybe I was frightened. And yet, this was important work, meaningful work.

Through Betsy and David and others, I encountered a different Jesus, whose power was not in good manners but in justice, in risk, and in being present. This Jesus was dangerous enough to be executed by the state. This Jesus drew me in and gave me a hunger for more. I did not know what to make of this longing or of the depth of feeling that awakened inside me on the shores of Guatemala's blood-drenched Lake Atitlan.

I was not imagining the church as my place or ministry as my work. I only knew that I still wanted to rescue people in burning buildings and cats caught in trees. I wanted someone to think my life had mattered; a greater truth is that *I* wanted to think it mattered.

We circled through Nicaragua and had meetings with Sandinista and Contra and Somozista and Presbyterian missionaries. That trip changed me, enraged me, and humbled me. The contours of my expectations and dreams shifted. I had left for Central America wanting to make a difference, wanting to be a good person. I believed that generosity was a most important thing. When we visited an orphanage, I commented to Dr. Shaw that these children, who were laughing heartily and using me as a jungle gym, tore at my heartstrings and made me want to take one home.

"You helped pay to make them orphans with your tax dollars," he said. "I suppose you've bought one or two."

Suddenly generosity was not as important as justice; kindness wasn't as important as truth. I returned from that trip weary with the knowledge that thousands of beautiful mountain-living people were dying in a land close to my own and that I, an American, was complicit in their deaths. This understanding shaped both my vision and my experience of

Jesus.

Our Nicaraguan and Guatemalan hosts exhorted us to go back and tell the truth, to be their voices. David Kaylor invited us to protest against the Contra war at the North Carolina Capitol in Raleigh a few weeks after we returned to the USA. I considered that heretofore I had been a "good girl" and had bowed to the expectations of my elders. I considered the application I had put forward to work as the first Service Coordinator of Davidson College and how much I wanted the position. This was a "nice" way of supporting the disadvantaged. Demonstrating at the Capitol would not be a "nice" approach. Protesting could be messy, in your face, and public. Could it be a strike against me for the job I wanted?

David Kaylor comfortably spoke to the media and marched in streets. I uncomfortably considered the measures of courage I lacked. I did not go to the protest. I got the position at Davidson College.

I had let Jesus down. Not only the Jesus of 2,000 years ago who was executed by the Roman government. I had also abandoned Jesus, the humble fisherman I'd met in a ramshackle hut in Santiago, Atitlan—whose name I could not record in case my journal was lost or stolen. I had let down Jesus, the wife, whose husband was castrated in front of her before having his fingernails removed and his arms and legs sawed off. That is the Jesus I let down because I was scared to visit the Capitol of Raleigh, NC and say, "Enough."

I did not go to seminary as penance for this betrayal. I went to seminary to find companions and courage. And I went carrying a keen interest in theology. Why do people believe what they do about the divine? Why are our images so limited? How can we build between our assumptions and the truly great mysteries of God? How can the gospel be told so that Christians will cease to allow the massacre of the poor?

I wanted to make the world a better place. But how? I had

considered social work. But I did not want to work for the government that was funding the Guatemalan death squads and the Contras. I did not want to fill out all those government forms. I wanted to make the world better because Jesus teaches us to pray, "Thy will be done on Earth as it is in Heaven."

I imagined seminary as a playground where I would play with ideas and prepare to make a difference for immigrants and other disenfranchised people. I expected seminary to give me language and insight to help me better tell the story of faith.

This decision was not easy or clear at the time. I also wanted to teach on an Indian reservation. I wanted to engage theology, but I still did not want to be a "minister." I was relieved when the Committee on Preparation for Ministry chair informed me that if I went to the Methodist Divinity School I had chosen, the Presbytery would "never ordain me." I was angry at this manipulative talk but I felt relieved for someone else to take responsibility for my struggle about ordained ministry. If the Presbytery would never ordain me, then I would not have to struggle with my call.

Duke Divinity School in the early 1990s provided an opportunity to focus on Liberation Theology and Christian Ethics. Dr. Fred Herzog (whose favorite theologian was the artist Paul Klee) taught Latin American liberation theology. Dr. Stanley Hauerwas taught the ethics of a peculiar and particular community that was pacifist and more interested in faithfulness than "rights." Dr. Mary McClintock Fulkerson gave clarity and focus to theology for and by women. Dr. Willie Jennings brought racism directly to the baptismal font. "When you get to your upper middle class white suburban church," he said to me one day, "I want you to take a child into your arms and baptize that child saying, 'I baptize you in the name of the Father, the Son, and the Holy Spirit. **You are no longer white.**'"

In the middle of my studies, I picked up and moved to Mexico to learn Spanish (and probably to revisit the ghosts of my earlier cowardice). I met Jorge Torres. He is not too serious about questions of God and Church if he entertains them at all. Jorge made a difference in the world. He built a language school to help Salvadoran refugees living in Mexico. I found Jorge's commitment to the poor admirable and was intrigued that his motivation had nothing to do with faith or religion. I was becoming serious about this liberation Jesus. I was getting serious about telling the gospel in a colorful and vibrant way that honored those Guatemalan faces and a white patent-leathered fireman girl.

Jorge and I had a lot of conversations about God and church. I wanted to know more about how one could make a difference outside the church. He wanted to know about a young woman who was a liberationist (like the Catholic church in Mexico at the time) and who wanted to become a "pastora." Only Protestants ordain women to be pastors/priests. And the Protestants in Mexico preached the promise of a salvation yet to come and did not engage in the liberationist movements of political consequence. The Catholic church did that. I would explain myself by saying that I was going to be a "pastora," but I believed in justice like the Catholic church. Jorge remained puzzled and intrigued that I was interested in becoming a "pastora" when I seemed to him so committed to liberation theology.

We visited the Guatemalan refugee camps in Comitan, on the Guatemalan/Mexican border. These are the camps that the families had moved to as the Guatemalan army claimed their land. The civil war had ended and they were being returned to their land. They were frightened. They begged me to return with them and stay for a short time to ensure their safety while they resettled. They did not have confidence that the war was really over or that they would be able to return to the land after their ten-year exile. I thought very seriously about it. I remembered my failure to give them voice at the Capitol in Raleigh. I wanted to be courageous enough to go with them, to forgo my Master of Divinity and to do something that would really matter for them, to give them comfort and to prevent their homes from being burned down again. I was afraid to go with them, afraid I would become more Guatemalan, have a Guatemalan family. I was not ready to never come home again. I took a cab to the airport instead.

Jorge rode with me to the airport. "I cannot believe you are going to go back to your country and wear a black robe and say the things that your priests say. You do not believe them."

Tears stained my journey home as I felt the weight and truth of his words.

I finished my master's degree. I bought a black robe. Jorge was right: there are things some men and women who wear them say that I do not believe. I do not believe in making the church better by purifying ourselves from the stench of the world. I do not believe in a God of wealth or comfort or complacency.

Every time I wrap the black robe about myself I feel the weight of Jorge's words. But I also feel the freedom of the gospel. "Do not be afraid. Do not fear, I am with you always." (Isaiah 43) I feel the opportunity to tell the gospel in a new and fresh way. I feel the opportunity to build community and to engage the Creator's world.

The union card I carry as an ordained clergywoman gets me through many doors where people's lives are burning down around them. It has gotten me into hospital rooms where death lurks and where fear grips people in that thin-veiled space between life here and life beyond. People have pounded laments into my ample back and screamed their questions of rage, fury and terror, '"Why??!" " Why did Jesus steal my baby?" "Why did my son get shot?" " Why did God let me drive my car into a tree and kill by baby girl?" "Why can my child not reach full term?"

For people who have burned quietly with scandals and sorrows and unspoken yearnings, my black robe has allowed them space for outpouring, a place to wonder, sometimes even freedom.

At first, I succumbed to the seductive notion that I was making a very big difference to those I met in the hospital and its waiting rooms. Soon I came to terms with the truth. In fact I was bearing witness to something holier and grander than I—it was that majesty and mystery that was making the difference. On the other hand, it would be disingenuous to suggest that who I am played no part at all. Other people wearing the same robe would undoubtedly kindle different responses and opportunities. My job was not to bring God into the room, but to show up and note how God was there. I learned that it is hard to be present to suffering, to stay in a room full of chaos and pain, to not leave when you cannot fix anything. God's willingness and capacity to stay in a room of suffering, no matter what, is what God's power came to mean to me. It wasn't about changing the outcome; it was about being present throughout.

As a hospital chaplain I learned to pray out loud and not protect God from failing people. I learned to offer the extraordinary longings and desires and fears and hopes in ordinary language toward all that is holy. I learned to listen to the spaces between words and actions and to wait for all that is holy to speak back. I was called to the room of a woman saying goodbye to her fourth miscarried baby. She had a scrapbook of pictures of the baby's sisters and brothers, and as she held the tiniest formed fetus she told her stories of each pregnancy and each dream. The nurses thought she was crazy. My mentor, Agnes Barry, thought her a great theologian. "Isn't that a wonderful image of Mother God?" Agnes said. "Maybe God also has a big book of pictures of all of us in the times we fail to hold on long enough, the times we abort the effort for life before it is time. Perhaps God fingers those pictures and remembers all that we've hoped for and failed at. And God loves us still."

Hospitals hold all walks of life. The impoverished woman—who grabbed her daughter, ran to the car to flee her abusive husband and then drove into a tree, killing her unbuckled toddler—comes to mind. I think of the accused murderer of an Oregon tourist who was shot by police and who died in my unit; he was an organ donor when no one believed "a family like that would give anything to anybody." There was the woman who wore across the top of her head a crown of staples that held her scalp together. A police dog had ripped her open during an armed robbery. She was a straight A student from a "good part of town" who had given her life over to heroine. Her mother visited daily. She is one of the most courageous and saddest women I have ever known.

I think of a wealthy woman who got her own private waiting room when her husband landed in the trauma unit after a car accident. She wore her pearls and furs every day but would not sit in a room with children from India. She was above all of that. I was outraged. One day as I complained of her arrogance a colleague, Chaplain Ron Case, adopted her persona: "Why won't you pray with me? I am scared too. Will you not sit with me because I have pearls and furs?" It turns out I had placed myself above her at about the same distance she positioned herself from Indian children. I have remembered this.

I once cottoned to the notion that God was mostly on the side of the poor and the very vulnerable. The bejeweled woman challenged that belief. Today I would say I suppose God has a preferential option for life. Whenever we are part of bringing, encouraging, inviting, protecting life we might be on God's preferred list. I would add, especially when we are fighting for life and abundance on behalf of the most vulnerable. This awareness matters to me. It has helped me integrate the fact of my privilege with the knowledge of its consequences for the poorest on our planet. It has given me some grace—to believe in the radical Jesus who tolerates neither the child made to starve nor the adult allowed to hoard.

God, I believe, is interested in life here on Earth, not only in the life we will live after we leave here. My theology has been shaped more by incarnation than atonement. I have been formed by the vision of human suffering I have encountered, by the laments of shattered dreams, and by the squalor of human living. I have not been moved by the notion that there will be some reward after this life; I am moved by the tenderness and power of compassion shared in this life. I have found God to be very present in the hospital corridors and in the bloodstained forests of the Lacondon jungle of Mexico. I truly see the face of Christ in the faces of children being carried by barefoot women in search of missing fathers in Chiapas and in the faces of those pasting photographs on the fence in front of the World Trade Center. I have been changed by a woman who was wearing pearls. I have been haunted by my lack of courage to camp with the refugees. I believe the poor are very relevant to this world. I believe God is moving in all things here and that we encounter God at many street corners and in many congregations.

I have been taught about incarnation from a mentally ill woman who exclaimed in a group that she was not only mentally ill, she was spiritually sick. She wanted to go to Church because she needed a hospital for her spirit. But she believed the churches she'd encountered didn't want her there; she felt she reminded them that they too might not be so spiritually well. She said the mental hospital was the only place she could go, but it didn't have the medicine for her spirit that it had for her mind.

I have been taught a great deal by incarcerated women. My most recent congregation was women living in prison and those recently released. The great majority of them are survivors of physical, sexual, economic abuse. Most of them are addicted to violent substances. Some of them are a challenge to love and difficult to like. They need, yet they are strong and beautiful and holy. They have taught me that liking each other is not necessary for ministry. They have taught me what survival means. They have shown me darker sides of incarnation than I would want to imagine. They have made redemption incarnate for me. They have given me an appreciation for atonement that focuses attention on the life after here – the life after suffering. In their gospel singing I saw them living, briefly, without suffering. They have shown me beauty in wretchedness. And they have shown me wretchedness in myself—when I was silent but should have spoken up, or when I choose the comfort of complacency over action. They have cast light and shadow on my desire to fix what, in my estimation, is broken. They have shown me the pain of my own impatience. They exhaust and depress me. And yet they sing. They dance. They pray. They draw. They write. They breathe in and out of the same oxygen we all breathe. They are part of us and we of them. They inspire me.

I remain unconcerned about Heaven or who goes there. I figure that is God's business. I am still more interested and moved by God's creation and who lives here. I am a convert to the wisdom of Julia Esquivel, a renowned Guatemalan poet. She once said to me, "I no longer believe in words. I believe in acts." This is quite a statement from a woman who lived in exile for many years because of the words she crafted and by which she stood, in defiance of her motherland's military rule.

It is not the words that I believe in so much as the space between the words, the negative space. It is the gasp at a well-spoken prayer, the track of a tear wetting the face of someone who has heard mystery in a sermon, the wide grin of a child giggling in the pew because it's not all so serious after all. It is not only the awesomeness of God but the incarnation, the walking around getting messy and dusty, and the sand-in-your-toes holiness that speaks to me.

Sometimes when I puzzle about how I came to be a priestess of this old religion, I hear my history in my veins. Both of my great grandfathers on my father's side were Presbyterian ministers. One of them lost his inheritance over it. My father's father was also a Presbyterian minister. My father did not want this trade. Dad built a bridge between past and present when he took us to the Brown Derby restaurant after church and asked us what we'd learned in Sunday School. "I don't really believe that only Christians go to heaven," he would start and we would get a revisionist theological lesson over burgers and fries. I learned that God might welcome Jewish people, too. The parents of the Jewish children my father life-guarded at the pool did more to put food on his table and get him through college—after his minister father died—than some of the Christians in his own church. I was never allowed to swallow church speak whole. I suppose my father, like me, also wanted to tell the gospel better.

At my ordination as a Minister of Word and Sacrament (it happened after all), my father remarked that I was not the child he thought would be a minister. It would have been my brother, David, whose ministry has been with adjudicated youth as an outdoorsman and as a guidance counselor for abused middle school children. My mother said her father was befuddled about the clergy. "Funny thing about some of those ministers" he is reported to have said, "some of them are right smart."

I grew up reading the journals of my great grandfather Craig. He was clerk of Synod and a local pastor in the Presbytery where I now serve. He and I would differ on many counts. In fact, when women got the right to vote, he expressed his dismay with his prayer that women would "do their duty and vote the wishes of their husbands." I dare say he and I would cancel one another's vote on many issues. Even so, I feel the privilege of following in his steps. I take pleasure in knowing that this man in my yellowed pages was here before me, holding the tradition, performing the rites and rituals in the way respectable to his time.

My great grandfather was a man of his time, as was his son.

During Southern Reconstruction, my great grandfather wrote wills that listed at length where the "slave girl Anna" would go upon the death of her former master. He wrote fearfully in 1898 about the racial uprising, which he called the "War in Wilmington, North Carolina." I have his preaching dickey framed; sometimes I worry that the religion I continue to nurture is being framed behind glass as well.

My grandfather quietly preached on the humanity of "Blacks" and took some professional consequences for his gentle prophetic stances. My ancestors' words embodied the racism, sexism, and provinciality of their time. I am proud of my heritage in their service and in the ways that they wished for a better world and a more faithful community. They worked for payment in pigs and chickens and kept careful records. They wrote the history of their own day for posterity, and they lived with integrity even as they were men of their day. They did not write of joy as much as of duty, or justice as much as of righteousness.

My father had many mixed feelings about church I think. He sat with my brothers and me every Sunday and took responsible leadership roles. But I think he, like me, did not believe some of the things the folks wearing the black robes said. He did not like the rules and regulations so much. He is a traditionalist in many ways, but in later years he really loves reading the new scholarship coming out and what the gospel might offer a larger world.

My mother loved the hymns her granny used to hum in the kitchen. I heard lots of lore about the courage of that great granny of mine who on awakening to read her Bible, startled a burglar and said, "Young man, does your mother know what you are doing right now?" He dropped the bag and ran away and great Granny got the stolen loot returned to its rightful owners. My mother volunteered in church, a place that welcomed both her creativity and her organizational skills. She wrote a grant to start the first homeless shelter in Tallahassee, Florida. She organized the Christmas International House sponsorship. Our Christmases were filled with Connie from China, who taught me to play Ping Pong, and with other young adults from all over the world. She and my father also advocated successfully for the first international mission trip my congregation ever took to Haiti in 1984.

My mother once joked with a friend that she didn't know why I always wanted to run off to other countries and help poor people. "I raised her to get married, have kids, and live in a nice house." I wasn't sure at the time if her words were a joke. But the look of concern on her friend's face, a look of shared disappointment as I saw it, made me believe her for years. I now know that she was proud of me and perhaps both envied and appreciated my adventurous life.

Growing up, I thought the activities in my church were both fun and worthy. On camping and mission trips, and leading worship in the choir (we had 100 youth in our choir), we were always made to feel loved and important. We believed it was possible to be good and to please God. Our youth leaders encouraged friendly pranks in the effort to build community. For me, church embraced love and laughter and joy even though those in the black robes often seemed somewhat grim and beleaguered.

I realized that by becoming a minister I was becoming my mother, the professional version. It's not always the words children hear as loud as the actions. I followed my parents' footsteps to the church, which had been a place both welcoming and wanting, and finally, with a radicalized vision of the biblical characters, the most interesting place I could imagine.

The church that first welcomed me to the baptismal font, funeral service, and communion table was Amity Presbyterian Church in Charlotte, NC. They entrusted their youth and children to me and bore up with my anxiety about preaching and my too seminary-ish way of talking. This congregation knew how to love and train ministers.

From there I moved to Selwyn Avenue, which opened its heart and arms to me. They blessed my voice, celebrated my love of words and children and liturgy. Worshipping there dazzled me with a vibrancy and pleasure I had not known before and have not felt since. This church invited me to join them on a mission to Mexico and allowed me to be the first woman (to our knowledge) to serve communion in that Yucatan Presbytery. These congregants knew what profound pleasure I took in this radical act.

I moved next to Chapel Hill, North Carolina, where I was called by University Presbyterian Church to be the Associate Pastor for Campus Ministry. I was responsible for Presbyterian ministry to UNC Chapel Hill and for the congregation's outreach ministries. In all three congregations, I noticed, the duties for outreach have fallen within the sphere of my purview. Many congregations grant the associate, rather than the senior pastor, the responsibilities for the larger community as well as the financial responsiveness to extra-congregational needs.

University Presbyterian Church further welcomed my voice and invited a more poetic approach to preaching and written prayer. My work there was predominantly programmatic and administrative. Campus Ministry was a delight to me. I could focus on education and programs and participate in telling the gospel story in new ways. Intellectual pursuits were valued and excellence in ministry was both expected and rewarded. In addition to all this, I was able to take students to protests in Washington, DC against the war in Iraq and to the vigils for peace at the School of the Americas at Fort Benning, Georgia. Walking with my students, carrying crosses with the names of massacred Guatemalans, felt like completing a circle of call from my own college days. I led mission trips and developed a preparation program for educational trips to Guatemala, Haiti,

Nicaragua, Cuba, and the Dominican Republic. Two of my former students spent a year doing ministry in Guatemala and continue to visit there. I did not expect to find, in the students for whom I was responsible, the courage and company I had been seeking in my own college years. But I did. I have felt their company as a blessing. I am grateful and amazed that the labyrinth-walk of ministry surprises us with déjà vu and patterns of grace.

I would still say that I do not see many of the black robes having much fun. I think the robe carries the burdens of high expectations, solemnity, and others' pain—just as it opens the doors of intimacy and presence. I find that most days I am having a fair share of joy and fun in the midst of ministry. I discover opportunities and challenges along the way and I am grateful for the privileges afforded high priestesses. I have no certainty as to whether my life will have mattered in any sort of ultimate way by the time of its twilight. I suspect buildings will still burn and cats will still get stuck in trees. Suffering and squalor will not have ended. Still, life is a great gift to me. Those who cross my path change me and enhance my vision and I am grateful for most of the things that have stretched and challenged me and reminded me to value joy.

Unlike many, I was not called by a voice or any certainty. Sometimes I even wake in the middle hours of the night and wonder if perhaps I've been an imposter all this time. Maybe I never was a priestess or a minister. Maybe I am still just a wannabe fireman who found a welcoming, familiar place to practice rescuing lost creatures and to soothe burns, including my own. Who is really ever to say?

Write About:

—Long black robes

—Party shoes

—Making a difference in the world

—Courage and cowardice

—Liberation Theology

—Incarnation vs Salvation

—Joy and ministry

—Ministry outside church

A Change of Life

Betty Berghaus

Over twenty years ago my husband died of cancer. He was only forty years old. I was thirty-six, and our daughter was almost seven. To say that my life changed irrevocably seems so obvious, but it is true. If a friend had told me then that in twenty years I would still be single and yet happy, I would have probably laughed in her face. If she had told me I'd be a minister, I would have been incredulous. A Christian educator is one thing, but a minister? Not for me. Or so I thought.

Church has always been important to my family. When I was five years old, my mother took me to Sunday School for the first time and tried to leave me there. I cried and cried, clinging to her. Finally the teacher said, "Harriet, why don't you stay and help me teach?" She did. The next year I moved on, but my mother stayed with the five-year-old class for the next thirteen years. I like to tell people that at an early age I started recruiting Christian educators.

When we were young, my sister Robbie and I would plan worship services for our family and friends. Sometimes Robbie would write out a bulletin of the service on construction paper. I remember reading Scriptures, singing hymns and praying, but I do not remember a sermon. If there was one, Robbie gave it because she was older and always in charge. When we sang, she sang soprano, and I was her backup and harmony. I was never the star and had no inclination to be in the limelight. Eventually Robbie stopped offering our homegrown worship services, but we continued to participate in church throughout our childhood.

A lot of people fall away from church in college. Once I had a car, though, I drove to an 11 o'clock service at a nearby

Presbyterian church. We also had a required chapel service once a week at college. One of my favorite professors, a small, proper British woman who taught English, pointed out to me that all of my papers focused on religious themes. I had not noticed until she said that. Even when I wasn't aware, faith was part of my life.

I graduated from college with an English degree and no real hopes or aspirations. My Southern belle mother told me that, as a woman in the mid-1970's, I could be a teacher, a bank teller, or a secretary. She also expected me to be married by the end of college. I was a bit lost. My sister suggested I apply to the Presbyterian School of Christian Education in Richmond, because she had gone there. I went for a year, and then took a year off from the two-year program, because I was unsure that I felt called to Christian Education.

I started working in a church in Florida, where I was living at the time; the church heard that I had training in Christian Education. Then and there, I felt the call of God. I loved the energy of the teens in the youth group that I led and the enthusiasm of the children in my multi-aged Sunday School class. I learned a lot about how churches work in our weekly staff meetings that were attended by every working member of the staff, from pastors to janitors. The next year I returned to graduate school with a new eagerness to finish my education and find a church position.

Then came something I was not expecting – I met a man at school, who knew he wanted to marry me and even had picked out a day and time for our wedding. Eventually we married and settled in Charlotte, North Carolina, where I worked as a director of Christian Education and Steve found a pastoral internship at another church. Our respective churches often asked us about each other. "Where's your husband?" "Your wife?" We were both so busy at our own jobs that we didn't have time to attend each other's churches.

In the fall of 1980, we moved back to Richmond so that Steve could finish his Doctorate of Ministry degree at Union Seminary. I worked at Cokesbury Bookstore downtown where I learned a lot about Christian Education resources. After Steve graduated, we went to a church in Durham, North Carolina, where he served as the only pastor, and I worked part-time as an educator. Together, Steve and I led the youth group.

Three years after we married, at Christmas time, we decided to try to have a baby. My father died the day after Christmas and in early January, we confirmed that I was pregnant. In February, Steve was diagnosed with Hodgkins Disease, a cancer of the lymph system. The oncologist assured us that he could be treated and cured by the time the baby was born. We had a daughter, Mary, in September of 1982.

Steve struggled with the cancer on and off for seven years. His church did not handle the illness very well. One family left because the church could not pray Steve well. The cancer was a struggle for us as well. I remember saying to Steve with frustration one day, "Why you? Why do you have cancer? You're young and good and have a family to raise and a good career as a pastor."

Steve said simply, "Why not me?"

Though Steve struggled and experienced some depression in the early years of his disease, his faith was always strong, stronger than mine. He led me to a deeper trust in God.

The pastor who had retired just before Steve came never left the area and never quit ministering to the members. He would call Steve to let him know that he had visited someone in the hospital or that he was going to do someone's funeral or wedding. In this way, he prevented Steve from ever becoming the pastor that the members had called. One year when Steve had to take time off from his position because of the severity of his cancer treatment, the church asked the retired pastor to serve as interim pastor.

About a year later, when Steve was well again and told the Session he was ready to go back to work, the Session asked him to co-pastor the church with the retired man. All of my training and experience in church polity told me that this was not a good situation. Feeling the pressures of working with the man who was supposed to be retired, Steve eventually left his church job and started attending the church where I was working.

I had taken a part-time position as a Director of Christian Education and was also working at the Presbytery office in the area of Christian Education. Now my two jobs were supporting our little family. Steve took classes at a technical college in computer and bookkeeping, and, because he was home more than I, served as the school parent for Mary until he died in 1989, just before Mary turned seven.

He died in the hospital, from renal failure, just as we were preparing to take him home with Hospice help. I was with him when he died, and I remember thinking at that moment: all we have is God and love – and that was enough. Verses from Romans 8 sustained me through Steve's illness, especially the verses telling us that when we do not know how to pray, the Spirit prays for us in groans too deep for words. After Steve's death, verse 28 became the driving force for my life: "We know that all things work for good for those who are called according to his purpose."

My part-time position at the church became full-time, perhaps because of the kindness of the church. The job went well until the pastor of forty years retired. The new pastor was less than an exemplary pastor or man, and less than honest. He undermined my job, and my position was eliminated—leaving me a single mom without a job, and depressed. I could have quit church at that point, but my Romans mantra and my desire for Mary to have a good church experience kept me going.

Mary and I started attending Westminster Presbyterian Church in Durham, North Carolina, and became very active there. Soon after we joined, we took part in the summer musical, dancing and singing with church members of all ages. Mary, with her gymnastics grace, was better than I at this, but we both got to know church members better during this lively experience. I also volunteered in the church office while unemployed. A church member from my former church helped me find a job as a receptionist for a sports publishing company. It brought home a paycheck, but I quickly realized this was not the type of work I wanted. I decided to train as a Stephen Minister at Westminster. I had felt an inner calling ever since Steve became sick – a call to a listening rather than an educational ministry. I continued to explore that calling, with a unit of Clinical Pastoral Education at a local hospital.

With some reluctance and fear about my ability to succeed in school, I finally applied to seminary and only to Duke Divinity School; I did not want to add to Mary's trauma by moving her from her home. Having not been an "A" student in college, I didn't expect to get into Duke. But my fifteen years of life experience must have helped, and God must have too, because I was accepted. I worked harder than I ever had at school, finally believing in what I was doing and where I was headed. Mary, who was in middle school by then, helped by learning to cook simple meals for us and by drilling me on my Greek and Hebrew flash cards. At the time, I thought, I would be a hospital chaplain, in order to help others dealing with illness and death.

While in school I worked for an urban ministry that helped families with rent, utilities, food, and medicine. I was also dealing with my mother, who lived in nearby Raleigh, North Carolina. She fell and broke a leg, and had a long hospital and rehab stay. I cleared her house of alcohol before she went home, since the doctor told her that clearly her drinking had led to the fall. She never drank again and I grew to admire her remarkable strength of character and her faith.

These were stressful years, to say the least. And yet I made the best grades I had ever made in any school, and passed all of the Presbyterian Church's ordination exams the first time through. God clearly had a path for me; I could not have done so well on my own.

When Westminster learned that for my Duke degree I had to serve an internship in a local church, the head pastor quickly said, "Then you'll do that here." So I became a student pastor at my own church. Soon after, the associate pastor left, and I stayed on to serve as an interim for his position in pastoral care. When a search committee was formed, I applied for the position as a full-time pastor. The Presbytery recommended that the church not call a member as a pastor. And yet, after a year's search, they called me.

I have been serving there ever since. This position has been a gift from God to me, I know, as I have grown to love that which I once most feared - preaching and leading worship —being in the limelight. I wanted to listen, and to walk others through the kind of tragedies that my family had endured, but I was not sure I had the skills needed to lead worship. Yet I slowly but surely became comfortable being a pastor. The congregation nurtured me. I began to welcome the opportunity to lead worship and pastor to people, walking with them from baptism through marriage and even to death.

I was happy in my work but still felt as if something were missing. I called it a need for "peace." This was my "holy longing," as Ronald Rolhauser calls it, a fire inside that needed fueling. I tried pastor support groups, but never found them particularly helpful. One day I met a Spiritual Advisor and started going to see her once a month. I still go. She listens to my stories and struggles and always directs me toward my relationship with God.

She told me early in our time together that I might come to crave daily spiritual time. I was skeptical at first but now relish my self-appointed period for solo reflection. I have not remarried. Within my church family and my Rehoboth colleagues, I have friends on whom I can call when I need to talk or to get away, and I am now happy in my personal life and professional life. I don't feel that longing anymore.

Change will come into every life; that is inevitable. And change can scare us, disrupt our plans, force us to, indeed, grow. But with the help of God, we can be assured that "all things work for good for those who love God, who are called according to God's purposes" (Romans 8:18). My mantra. We walk this way together. Thanks be to God!

Write About:

—Childhood rituals having to do with church

—A death in the family

—Stephen Ministry

—Co-pastoring a church

—Your private spiritual life

Searching for Home

Katie Ricks

As the daughter of an Army officer, I moved every two to three years. This was a pattern lived by my dad's family and his dad's family. A consistent home base and friends you've known since you began to walk are not my family's traditions. We traveled, met lots of people, and got a broad view of the world. My parents cultivated within us a keen interest in learning, a curiosity about how things work, and a desire to understand other people and the cultures and backgrounds from which they came.

The most important task for my parents, upon hearing of a new assignment, involved locating the best public schools and a good church for us to join. Lucky for me, these were my two favorite activities. The consistency and structure of school and of worship within the Presbyterian tradition grounded me.

When I was baptized, those who gathered took vows on behalf of the entire Christian community. So, those who were present—and everyone I encountered growing up and still encounter today—were responsible for nurturing me and raising me to know and live God's Love. From an early age, I appreciated the strength of those baptismal vows.

As we came to worship at each new congregation, I already knew the rhythms, the order, the music, the liturgy. I knew that God loved me, in fact that God loves everyone. And I trusted that the people in church would take care of me and love me and teach me.

They did.

And I did everything I could do in church. I attended and taught Sunday school, worshipped, sang in the choir, raked leaves, fixed up homes for people in need, attended youth group, and went to church camp and conferences. In high school I was ordained a deacon and put in charge of the annual church picnic.

Church was home for me. It was the place I felt most comfortable; it was the place that I, a shy child, spoke and taught and shared. When I wasn't in church, I always felt awkward and unsure about myself. I never felt connected to who I was or who others were. I just never felt like I was in the right skin. Church was where I knew I belonged, even in the torturous years of adolescence. And in college, when I wasn't consistently a part of a faith community, the strength of the God I knew and had learned about as a child sustained me and centered me as I sought to figure out who I was.

Just after college, a new understanding of who I was began to reveal itself. I wasn't rebelling; I wasn't experimenting; I wasn't seeking a "different lifestyle." I was just finding ways to maneuver through life, trying to figure out what I was supposed to do when I grew up. And, in that time, I came to realize that I am gay.

Sitting here sixteen years later the realization seems almost insignificant, but then it was huge. I knew society wasn't keen on gay people, and I knew the church wasn't either. The one thing that held me during the struggle of "coming out" was that I knew God loved me and walked with me – the church people had taught me well.

I tried to deny being gay, ignore it, push it away, but the thing was, for the first time, I felt like a whole person. I started to understand myself and others and the world better. I stopped watching myself from the outside and felt like I could dwell within my own body.

With this new-found understanding of self, I moved to the South, found a job in residence life and counseling at a school in rural Georgia, and decided it was time to return to church. In this wee little Southern town, the minister at the Presbyterian

Church happened to be a woman, which somehow made the thought of getting back into a faith community easier. As soon as I sat down in the small, ornate, wooden sanctuary, I knew I had found home again. I kept feeling pulled into that space, into that community, into the presence of God. I heard God telling me that this was where I was supposed to be.

In my work at the college, I encountered young adults who were struggling deeply with events and transitions in their lives. Many of them, though, had not grown up surrounded and strengthened by communities of faith that bathed them in God's Love. They had nothing to sustain them and guide them and remind them that they were not alone. I realized I could not provide care and counseling to them without talking of faith. Since that kind of conversation is prohibited at state institutions, I felt an aching within me – a deep yearning to provide a space for young people to experience and be buoyed by the Love of God, so they would know that they never walked alone.

I began to feel a tug towards ministry. The pull grew stronger and stronger until I could not deny it or push it away, despite the huge obstacles that were certain to arise. You see, at the exact time I was feeling this calling to ministry, the Presbyterian Church was formally inserting into its constitution the prohibition of the ordination of lesbian, gay, bisexual, and transgender persons.

In preparation for entering seminary, I moved to Atlanta, changed jobs, and began taking lay classes at Columbia Seminary. I found a great little church whose members reminded me that God loved me and walked along the journey with me; they elected to ordain me to serve as an elder in their midst; and they encouraged and sought to cultivate God's call within me. They were the palpable presence of God that I needed as I began this difficult journey.

The first hurdle for me was filling out the application to seminary. In an essay about my faith journey, I couldn't leave out the fact that I was a lesbian. I needed the school to know because I didn't want to lie, and I didn't want to have to watch and hide my every move. And yet, I didn't want my sexuality to become the focus. It was just a part of who I was. I wrote and deleted and yelled at the computer. Everything I produced seemed forced. I felt like I existed outside of myself again.

On the Saturday night before the application was due, I was angry and frustrated.. I alternated between throwing pillows, continuing to yell at the computer, and curling up in the fetal position on my bed. I had reached my breaking point. As was my practice then – I've made better choices since – I went for a drive in the middle of the night. I rolled down the windows and screamed and yelled, "God, you got me into this. You told me that you wanted me to be honest, and yet you're not giving me the words I need. This is your thing. You've got to show me what to do."

The tears and wind blew across my face and then, calm. At 1:00 AM, I felt surrounded – literally held – by God, and God said to me clearly, "Go home. Go to sleep. It will all be OK in the morning." And so I did. In complete silence, I drove home, crawled into bed and slept for the first time in weeks. I woke up refreshed and excited, anticipating the promise that was waiting for me.

That morning a woman named Janie Spahr was scheduled to preach at our church. She is a minister who is an "out" lesbian; she traveled the country preaching the Good News and working for the full inclusion of LGBT people in the church. Though I had never met her, I was to be her chauffeur for the morning. On the way to church, we exchanged light pleasantries about where we were from. Nothing personal.

When she stood up to preach the sermon, she said, "Well, I prepared a different sermon for today, but at 1:00 AM, God woke me up and told me I needed to tell stories, stories about people who have 'come out' and continued to serve the church."

I listened in sheer awe to the next half hour of stories about people just like me. After worship, church members who only knew I was preparing for seminary, not about the struggle I was having, came up to me saying, "She preached that sermon for you." I went home that afternoon and completed my essays with no difficulty. Indeed, the Spirit was alive and active in the world!

This encounter with God was the confirming moment for me of my call to ministry. As the struggles and joys continued throughout seminary, the grace of that moment continued to surround me.

Because I had grown up with such a deep sense of the church as my home – the place where I could most be myself – I assumed that the church would continue to welcome me with open arms. I didn't expect the tension and politics on the national level to impact my life directly. As I approached the Presbytery committee to begin my ordination process, I assumed everybody would see that I was just like others who were on the same journey. I thought they'd be willing to set aside the piece about my being gay.

The experience could not have been farther from my hopes. After a very supportive preliminary meeting with the committee, everything went downhill. They never asked me about my faith, my call, my growth in the church. They never asked what I was learning in seminary and how it challenged or strengthened my faith. They never said, "Welcome home; we're glad you're here." All they wanted to know about was sex – whether or not I was having any.

As the years of being "under the care" of the Committee on Preparation for Ministry progressed, I moved from overflowing tears to uncharted anger to pity for them and for the church. I have come to realize, in my best moments, that this isn't really about me. They are fighting the larger church battles *through* me, that what they say or think or imagine isn't *about* me. I am sitting in front of them, yet they do not see me; they see the "issue" they are fighting for or against.

The thing is, as long as I didn't have to deal with the greater church, I loved seminary. I was truly in the right place, and I had made the right decision to follow God's lead to be "out." My faith and my understanding of God became so much deeper because I was studying and exploring with my whole self, through the fullness of how God had created me. I developed deep relationships with people in ways I had never experienced before. I had opportunities to travel to amazing places and serve a fine church in downtown Atlanta. I learned to rely on other people and came to trust again this church that I called home. Being honest about all of me opened me to the fullness of joy and pain and struggle and love.

Until then my life had always been about flying under the radar. I would never have engaged in anything – intentionally or otherwise – that called attention to me, challenged a system, or caused others to not like me. God had called me to something different though, that I would never have done on my own. God called me to believe and live into my identity as a beloved child of God–wherever that might take me.

I worked at Central Presbyterian Church for two and a half years during seminary; they just kept designing new internships for me, so I could keep working there. The congregation encouraged me to learn and grow. They honored and affirmed my call to ministry and kept providing me with opportunities.

I learned a lot about the inner workings of the denomination. I saw the challenges encountered by those in power and the struggles they faced between their personal beliefs and their responsibility – perceived *and* real – to maintain the "peace, unity, and purity" of the church. The head of staff, Ted, and I developed deep respect and love for each other, nurtured by serving the community and leading worship together. Together we sought ways to navigate a Church that welcomed me and a denomination that did not.

In my last year there, I found myself caught in the middle of Ted's internal debates. My partner Paula and I had decided to have a covenant union ceremony. Initially, when I told Ted, he was thrilled. He offered to officiate the ceremony and host it at Central. "I don't want to push you or assume I would be the person," he said over breakfast one morning. "But I would love to do that, if that's what you decide."

Paula and I wrestled with this. We wanted to have the service "in the round," which wouldn't work at Central. But there was something special, of course, about having it at the church where I served and about Ted's offering—he was usually quite cautious. After much deliberation, we decided on Central and on Ted and told him.

That's when Ted told us he was going to have to rescind his offer. He was very apologetic and felt very bad. I was convinced that he did feel terrible. Still, he had offered and then reneged. He had gotten caught up in, and shut down by, the tension within the church.

We had an incredible worship service at the Friends Meeting House a few blocks from our house. It was in the round with over 200 people singing and celebrating with us. This ceremony was exactly what a wedding was supposed to be – a community affair. Our friends officiated – including an ordained Presbyterian minister and preaching professor who will preach my ordination one day. Friends arranged the flowers, played music, sang, and cooked the food for the reception. Ted and his family were there, and they celebrated just as raucously as everyone else. I wouldn't have wanted it any other way.

After seminary, God called me to serve at the Church of Reconciliation, nick-named "the Rec," in Chapel Hill, North Carolina. At the interview with them, I was comforted by the fact that they treated me like a normal person. I wasn't a token or an anomaly; they saw me simply for who I was. They asked me about my faith and how I could serve their congregation, about my strengths and weaknesses, about my hopes and dreams. They never asked about sex. They welcomed my partner and me – assisting with settling in, providing meals, and checking in regularly to see how we were doing. From the very beginning, I knew I had found a new home.

I have served the Rec for seven years now – a time filled with lots of learning and joy and frustration and burn out and love. My first Christmas Eve there, I looked out into the congregation while we were singing and saw each person individually. I remembered the stories they had shared, the projects we had worked on, the struggles they continued to wrestle with, and I realized that in Seminary they never told us that we would fall in love with the people in our churches.

This is a unique congregation, one that lives the Gospel in concrete ways. The Rec was founded in the late 1960's as a church dedicated to seeking racial reconciliation; ever since, it has sought to continue welcoming all who have come. They are committed to peacemaking and social justice as well as to deep sustaining worship and equipping folks for the journey of service.

This community, for the most part, is confident in its calling to serve the people of God – ALL the people of God – with justice and love. They are not shy about this either. In its best moments, the Rec has taught me that conflict of the healthy variety – open and honest disagreement – is welcomed and good. The congregation expects people, including the pastors, to share their thoughts, their feelings, their inner struggles, and their concerns within the church community. This way of being has encouraged me to continue working towards valuing my place, my opinions, my self in the world.

They have also taught me about Sabbath rest. As a recovering workaholic (I'm genetically predisposed) I've learned from them in subtle and not so subtle ways that God actually did take that commandment seriously. They honor my Sabbath day and challenge me when I opt not to honor it myself. They have told me they don't want me to work all the time, and they provided for a three-month sabbatical rest that I took in the summer of 2008. The sabbatical could not have come at a better time, as the previous year and a half had been a huge challenge to my calling.

On January 19, 2007, I gave birth to my daughter. It was the most profound experience of the miracle and power of God. I truly believe that I came face-to-face with God as Jordan entered the world. And her presence has continued to show God's love. She has taught me again to wonder, to explore, to learn. She has taught me to be present to what is going on at this moment. She has taught me that I control nothing, that God – and occasionally a toddler – guide and direct all that happens in the world. It's my job to be open to being guided. In my best moments, I remember what she and God have taught me.

When I first returned to work after having Jordan, the sadness about having to leave her in day care, the confusion about how to work when I had greater family priorities as well as significant post-partum depression, caused me great angst, frustration, and burn out. Add into that mix a major crisis in the youth group – a primary responsibility of mine – and I was spent. I felt trapped by my tasks at work and by the financial needs of my family. Except for times with Jordan, I was unable to see God's presence in the world. Everything was frustrating, and there was no way I could even come close to sensing a call to anything. I just went through the motions – hoping, trusting that things would come together eventually.

Some light began peeking through in the spring before my Sabbatical. I realized I liked my job again. I wasn't sure of my calling, but I didn't feel trapped anymore. Almost as quickly as things had collapsed around me, they opened up again, with a sense of newness and grace. And then the sabbatical offered time to enjoy the life that was emerging within and around me.

At one point during my sabbatical, I decided to prune the huge bushes in front of our house – a task I had no clue how to do, which is why they were six years overgrown. I started out slowly but eventually began cutting everything away. As I wrestled with the branches and clipped and pulled and clipped some more, I realized that my sabbatical was like my high-powered pruning session—an opportunity to cut away at strong, old patterns and ways of being in the world.

I wasn't sure the plants would survive the "pruning," but sure enough, a few weeks later, new growth appeared. The same has been true of my return to work. I don't feel the same as I did before. There is less baggage weighing me down, and I have a greater sense of being strengthened by my faith and by the love of my family. I am focusing on being with people, on intentionally spending time sitting with God, and on letting some of the details go by the wayside. Life seems less hectic now. I breathe more slowly. I laugh more. New growth is starting to appear. And renewed struggles.

"Tension is the arena of the Holy Spirit," states the 1983 *Historic Principles, Conscience and Church Government*. This is the document that the Presbyterians adopted when the Northern and Southern churches reunited after a 122-year split over slavery. *Tension* is a mild term for the state of the denomination right now.

I waver between deep love and compassion for and deep frustration and anger at my fellow Presbyterians. The prohibition of the full participation of lesbian, gay, bisexual, and transgender people in the church is in direct contrast with our core identity. Presbyterians were the ones who taught me that God loves everyone – everyone! There was never any doubt in my mind about that growing up. There was never any doubt in my mind about that when I "came out." I knew that God loved me – fully, completely, unconditionally. I have no doubt about that now.

What I doubt is the love of my fellow brothers and sisters in Christ. I hear them say that they love me deeply, and that is why they feel compelled to tell me that I am going to go to hell if I don't repent. We can break bread together and study together and pray together and laugh about our children's antics together, but they are not willing for us to serve together. I just don't get it.

Yet, when I start to rant about the people "on the other side," I see Ryan's face. I think about his family, about the sacrifices he and his wife have made to raise their four children from two different continents. I think about what good people they are, but he cannot budge with me. Instead, after months of gathering together, he stood up beside me to speak on the floor of the Presbytery. He talked about what an abomination gay people are and then said, "But, surely we should allow them into the church," as he awkwardly tried to put his arm around me.

I thought of Judas kissing Jesus in Gethsemane. I'm not Jesus, of course, and not going to be crucified – physically, at least. It's the betrayal – the betrayal of trust and relationship. I do not question Ryan's faith; he is clearly committed. And, yet, I do not understand his position.

Ryan is not the only one. I think of Jonathan, with whom I worked on seminary projects and traveled the Middle East. He even bought Cuban cigars for us to smoke together in Damascus, Syria on my 30th birthday. When I asked him if he was going to come to our covenant union ceremony, he said he just couldn't support that kind of sinful behavior.

What? How can they not really know who I am after all this time? Do they not see me? That's really what I want. I want them to take off the blinders through which they look at this "lesbian" and see me, Katie. I want them to see that I have been dipped into the same baptismal waters. I have attended the same churches and conferences and schools. I have wrestled with theologians and preaching professors. I have struggled with the reality of poverty and violence and sin in the world. We are the same – the same beloved Children of God.

I do not feel any less tension about folks who actually want me to be ordained. The thing is, they want a poster child – a banner to hold up. They want me to fight at all costs and lay down my life for the movement. They want me to support the annual onslaught of overtures and voting, and they want me to speak out against those who do not agree.

"Isn't there a bigger picture?" I ask. "Shouldn't we be providing care for folks who are going through this process?" This journey is hard. It is isolating and painful. Over time, I've realized that you can't implement a plan for caring that supports everyone. But, it seems to me that the conversation should focus on spirituality, not strategy. If we begin and end with worship and prayer and testimony about the presence of God, the strength to continue on is most assuredly there.

Strategy, in my mind, has no place in the church. It's slimy and sneaky and disingenuous I understand strategy in politics. But in the church? The place where we are all One? No, this is not the place for strategy. This is the place for honesty – honest sharing and honest listening. If we can't do that here, then it can't be done.

The debate has become more about power than anything else. Trust is long gone. Anxiety and fear are the emotions of the day – on all sides of the conversation. And in the meantime, those of us who are waiting at the door are left stranded while everyone else swirls around.

A new amendment came up for vote this year. The wording was different from the usual; it offered something that lots of people could get behind. All the organizations that are seeking the ordination of LGBT people worked together this time. In the past, they engaged in power struggles among themselves. The cooperative effort was a terrific victory. Great strides were made in the numbers of people voting yes, but the amendment was defeated – yet again.

Even with all the positives, the defeat feels exactly the same. It is a defeat. I am frustrated, angry, and apathetic - all at the same time. I'm not sure how one can hold all those emotions but here I am.

The amendment was defeated on a Saturday. The next morning in worship one of our members stood up to "announce" the results, and the experience of that was almost as disconcerting as the vote itself.

First of all, the defeat of the amendment doesn't belong with church "announcements;" it's a prayer concern. Then he said, "I have some bad news and some good news. The bad news is that the amendment failed [audible gasp], and the good news is that the numbers are so very close. So many people have changed their minds [nodding heads]."

Straight people need to know their work was not in vain. I get that. I really do, but that's really not good news to me. This is yet another time where LGBT people's worthiness as human beings has been debated across the country and the decision has been unfavorable. The Presbyterians who nurtured and raised me taught me that these Presbyterians (the same ones, mind you) are wrong – therapy has also helped. But, it's still the same message over and over and over and over again.

So, after I got slightly choked up by this member's comments, I still had to lead worship. I didn't know before showing up that I was supposed to read scripture that day - typical for the Rec, but after 7 years I can handle the surprise. The text I was to read was Romans 8, "nothing can separate us from the love of God." I had read this text a number of times. I skimmed it again before standing up, finding it unremarkable. Certainly, it *is* remarkable, but I was reading it cognitively. When I stood up, I experienced the Holy Spirit taking over me and the text and the space. It's hard to explain what happens when the text comes alive. The words come out of my mouth slower. I am hearing and listening to them at the same time that I am reading them. The call and response nature of the text drew me in as the caller and responder. "If God is for us, who can stand against us...Who is the judge? Jesus – the one who died for us and prays for us... Can anything separate us from the love of God?... NO!!! Nothing... absolutely NOTHING can separate us from the love of God in Christ Jesus our Lord."

THAT is the good news.

Higher vote tallies for the amendment may be good news for straight people. The Good News for me is that nothing separates us from the Love of God in Christ Jesus our Lord.

When I first started working with a Jungian analyst, I learned about the mandorla. The mandorla is the "almond" shape formed when two circles overlap. This ancient symbol is representative of the intersection of polar opposites. It's not a blending of the two, or a compromise. It is dynamic space – a place where new life emerges from the tension.

The fish symbol that Christians use to represent Jesus is in fact a mandorla. Jesus is the ultimate example. For He *is* the new life that emerges from the intersection of heaven and earth, God and humanity, spirit and flesh.

Through my struggles to find a place in this church that I used to call home, the mandorla has become a source of comfort and strength. It reminds me that the tension and pressure and angst take me to a new – or renewed – place. As I continue along this journey of faith, of life, of call, I pray for the courage to dwell in the mandorla. It is, after all, my home.

Write About:

—Feeling whole

—The church as home

—Dissent within your denomination

—Not being seen for you really are

—Sexuality and church

—Youth Ministry

—Doubt

—Pruning

—Sabbath

A Potter's Story

Cely Chicurel

The word which came to Jeremiah from the Lord: "Arise and go down to the potter's house, and there I will cause you to hear My words." So I went down to the potter's house, and there he was working at his wheel. And the vessel he was making of clay was spoiled in the potter's hand, and he reworked it into another vessel, as it seemed good to the potter to do.

Then the words of the Lord came to me: "Oh house of Israel, can I not do with you as this potter has done?" says the Lord. "Behold, like the clay in the potter's hand, so are you in my hand, O house of Israel."
Jeremiah 18:1-6

My younger brother, Chris, and sister, Catherine, and I would certainly say that we were raised in a loving Christian home. My parents were members of University Presbyterian Church, in Chapel Hill, North Carolina, and were very involved with all aspects of church life, from being choir members to church deacons. I have carried the mark of baptism with me throughout my life journey and the assurance of their faith has lighted my path.

I attended Sunday School as a child, went through Confirmation class, and learned all the church creeds. I believed that God existed and that Jesus was God's son; that belief, however, did not make me happy. Instead I felt that God was a distant and demanding judge, who created us but left us on our own to struggle along as best we could. Why was there so much suffering? If God was a loving Father, he was surely on extended vacation or he just didn't care about our problems. My parents were always reminding us to be thankful for the life we had, and I was. But I never felt close to the God of my childhood. I felt that there was a piece missing from my understanding, some commitment not made that would give my faith an assurance it lacked.

Grade school in Chapel Hill was hard for me. I was a slow reader and had to wear glasses in the second grade to see the board. Also I was easily distracted. My mind would often wander from the class work we were doing inside to the living world outside my window. I noticed the freedom of the squirrels, as they raced from tree to tree chasing each other, and wanted to join them. A bird's nest outside the classroom made me long to see if there were eggs inside. Some days the trees beckoned me through the opened school windows, and I wanted to escape, to climb high up in their branches.

After I learned to read I could not get enough of animal, adventure, and Nancy Drew stories. I would read under the covers with a flashlight long into the night. I had a wild and vivid imagination and entertained my family with my dreams every morning before school. I would make fairy villages with acorns, moss, and mushrooms or create a playhouse from sticks and Johnson grass. Our front yard hammock could easily become a boat that carried my friends on adventures. I was a well-liked and happy child, if a little shy, and was never disruptive in class. If the world of make-believe was almost real for me, so the natural world was magical and wondrous, full of beauty, and stimulating to all my senses.

During the summers we would visit my maternal grand-mother, Annie West Cely, in South Carolina while my dad taught summer school at the university. During the academic year, he was on the music faculty in Chapel Hill. Uncle Willy, mom's big brother, had a farm outside of Greenville and I spent many happy hours floating on his lake or wandering around the surrounding woods with my siblings, making up stories and enjoying the out-of-doors. My mother let us have complete freedom on the farm; every day was an adventure. Summer camps were also part of my childhood. While I struggled to fit into traditional school classrooms, I excelled in the outdoor camp setting. I learned to appreciate nature and love hiking and swimming. I felt close to all creation, especially the wild animals.

My room at home soon became full of all kinds of furry and not so furry creatures, from mice and hamsters to turtles and snakes. I cared for all my pets with dedication and devotion. The more I was drawn into the natural world, the more I felt distanced from the stressful world of humans. In my early teens I was labeled a distracted dreamer. I grew increasingly shy, retreating into a world of mystery books and science fiction.

I sometimes felt I could almost talk to God and would often verbalize my thoughts out loud as I walked along. But there were also times I felt so unhappy with myself that I couldn't believe God would ever love me. I had a real fear that God wanted more of me than I could give, and that if I ever gave in and said yes to this demanding God I would be consumed and lose myself. I contemplated mission work and even considered becoming a nun. I felt that one needed to give up everything to feel the approval of God. I believed in God but I also feared God and hated myself and hated the way God had abandoned the world. If God were so all-powerful, as I believed he was, how could he let pain and suffering continue? Why not just fix everything and let us all be happy.

I was often so miserable that I would long to just slip away into the woods and disappear. As a senior in high school I became so depressed that I dropped out of school and got a job in our local pet store. It was during these turbulent teen years that I grew away from the church. I rejected easy words of faith as I became more and more critical of the hypocrisy of church members, especially my parents. How could I believe what the church said if the church was full of "sinners" who didn't practice what they preached? I struggled with low self-esteem and anxiety. I could not accept that I was a person of worth.

Nothing I said or did seemed right. Every mistake, no matter how small, I took to heart. I wanted so much to be perfect but knew I failed daily to control my thoughts or actions. I was trapped in the dead-end trail of "works righteousness" and had no way to get out.

I don't know what would have happened if I hadn't been given the invitation to work with clay. My parents encouraged me to attend a small experimental community art center where I met a local potter named Dorothy Davis. With her help I discovered a magical connection between my love of animals, my imagination, and the clay. Like Jeremiah's, my visit to the potter's house was a moment of inspiration and discovery. I could think three-dimensionally and that proved an asset for sculpture work. I had a talent for art. Clay became the key to unlock the prison of my low self-esteem. I began to make little animal caricatures that were whimsical, friendly, and cute. I could bring magical worlds alive with clay, and to my amazement other people were interested in buying what I made. With the money I made working at the pet store and selling my pottery, I bought my first kiln, kick wheel, and all the supplies needed to set up a small pottery shop in my parents' basement. I finished high school by correspondence course and decided to go to college and major in art.

I headed off to college at Virginia Commonwealth University, ready to become an artist/teacher. But I was diverted when I fell in love with my first real boy friend, Donald Langlas, and returned home to Chapel Hill after only one year to get married. While Donald continued his studies at UNC, I got a job to help pay the bills. My husband became my "god" and I opened my heart to him, giving him all my love and devotion. Unfortunately, he was only human and betrayed my trust.

After three years and many counseling sessions, it was clear that our marriage was over. His path was not my path; I was not the one he wanted to be with. I was devastated. Alone and broken from the pain of betrayal and divorce, I enrolled in East Tennessee State University as a pottery major, ready to pick up the pieces of my life and continue on my journey alone. But there was to be a surprise in this turn of my life's journey.

The first Sunday in October, 1974, I went into the only Presbyterian Church in Johnson City, Tennessee. I went less to meet God and more because it felt like a nice thing to do. All those years as a child had left an impression on me. I had been at school for two and a half months and when Sunday morning came I felt like I needed to be in church. This one Sunday happened to be Laity Sunday and instead of regular Sunday School classes, all the groups were meeting together. Everyone was excited and energized because of their week-long revival. I felt a little out of place.

The joy of the people around me was unmistakable. When someone asked me, "Do you know Jesus Christ as your personal savior?" I was a little confused. This was not a question I had been asked at my home church. I responded that I was Presbyterian and had attended church as a child, but I really didn't know what they were talking about. I didn't have anything personal to tell them. My church was very academic and you either believed in Jesus as God's son or not.

When we went into worship I was hoping to regain my balance and just sit and listen, but things got stranger. The service was all about how you could have a personal relationship with Jesus and intimately know God. These people didn't sound like Presbyterians to me! I was afraid that I was no longer in a safe mainline church.

Knowing there was a God was one thing, but no one had ever talked about knowing God personally. I remembered how I had always felt that there was something missing in my faith and this personal part must be what it was. I rightly recognized that this could be a step that would change me, and I grew more fearful. I knew that deep down I was not happy. I had messed up my life doing things on my own. I had failed at love and didn't quite trust people or organized religion to fix things. I wanted more from God, but what would God demand of me? I didn't want to give myself away completely.

Then suddenly, as I was intellectually struggling with all these questions, God was there with me. The moment came as we stood to sing a song, a song that spoke directly to me. This one song began: "Have thine own way, Lord, have thine own way. Thou art the Potter, I am the clay. Take me and mold me after thy will, as I stand waiting, yielded and still." The words and their deeper meaning broke through all my questions and fears and told me who I was, who God was, and what I had to do. I felt alone and totally exposed. My heart turned over and I fell in love completely and forever with my Creator, the Master Potter.

I visualized myself as the clay, the inert earth material that needed shaping. I knew all about clay: How hard rocks were decomposed over time and became soft plastic clay. How the potter then dug up the clay from the ground. How the impurities and sticks were removed and the clay made ready to work. How strong hands had to work the clay, kneading and wedging it into shape, and finally placing the lump on the potter's wheel ready to shape. I felt the roughness of my own heart being smoothed out as I yielded my life in that one instant to God's strong knowing hands. I remembered how hard it was to center a piece of clay and I imagined God's concentration and patience as my life wobbled and twisted and finally came into center.

All parts of my life, my heart, head, and body surrendered that day. I finally accepted who I was. I understood the care a potter takes choosing the shape of each pot. I knew that a potter could not be distant from what was being formed on the wheel. God's hands had chosen me and touched me directly. I could either accept and become a finished person or fight it and remain nothing.

I realized that I was crying. A stranger who stood beside me reached over to touch me. My internal will was broken but there was more to come. The preacher asked anyone who had felt the presence of the Holy Spirit to come forward and kneel in prayer. My legs didn't want to move. I wanted to keep this experience between God and me, but I had said yes to the God of Creation and knew that to stay in my row and not to go forward was to deny my very existence. I went to the altar and for the first time truly opened my heart in prayer. God was real, God could be experienced because God had first chosen and touched me. Now began a long journey of faith through a second birth and baptism while I walked in fellowship with other Christians and grew in my knowledge of God's written word.

I finished college at ETSU as a pottery major. While I was in Tennessee I met Bill Chicurel, a devout Jew, who had just had a similar transforming faith experience; he had also just accepted Jesus as Lord. We connected on a very deep level and Bill became my forever soul mate. We returned to Chapel Hill and married in 1978. Soon afterwards we moved to Colorado where Bill was working on his doctorate in Music. In 1979 Miriam Ruth, our daughter, was born and two years later we moved back to Chapel Hill where our son, Joel Isaac, was born. But little Joel only lived for a few hours and for a while our journey took us through a very dark valley as we grieved his death. In 1982 Matthew Aaron, a true "Gift from God," was born and we rejoiced!

During the next long stretch of my life's journey, Bill worked for the post office and also took a job as music director at Orange United Methodist Church. I worked at home as a production potter and taught classes while raising our two children. In 1998 I answered a long time calling to Ministry and entered Duke Divinity School, where I completed a Masters in Church Ministry. I began a seven-year period as Christian Educator at

Orange Methodist.

When Bill retired in 2003 with diabetic induced disabilities, we needed to rethink our finances and needed a reliable income; we wanted to work together. Building on our gifts and strengths, we began an arts after school program in our home. We called our growing home-based business "Cely's House" and developed an assortment of community offerings including pottery classes, birthday parties, after-school programs, summer art camps, teacher workdays, spiritual retreats, and even piano classes taught by Bill. We are in the process of expanding to a larger wooded lot, where we can continue to connect children and adults to nature and the arts.

It has been more than thirty years since that Aldersgate moment in Tennessee and I am still moved by the image of God as my potter. I still affirm God's will over my own as I sing "Have Thine Own Way." I still come forward to kneel at the altar when I feel God's hand touching me and I respond with joy and not with fear. As I look back on my life and see all the twists and turns of my journey, I can clearly see God's presence moving with me as I travel. I can see God comforting me during the sad times and bringing people to me as helpers and guides when I was close to losing my way. I can see how God encouraged me to discover my special gifts with art and children and led me into teaching. God gave me Kingdom work to do as well in the Methodist Church.

I know that every choice I make either draws me closer to God or puts me out of center. But God is never far off. The God of the universe wants to be known by us and is constantly reaching out, seeking an opening to our hearts—a way to connect with us.

Each of us has a story to tell. My story is the story of a potter who, like Jeremiah, went down to the Potter's House and discovered the Word of God.

Write About:

—Scripture that holds profound meaning for you

—Your experience of nature as a child

—How does the natural world inform your life and faith now?

—God's relationship to human suffering

—Hypocrisy in the church

—Self esteem

—Being consumed by God

—Art and other creative outlets

Life at the Crossroads

Debbie Kirk

"Crossroads" has been a defining metaphor for me throughout my life. Decisions large and small about which road to take are pivotal in my faith journey. Do I go straight where I can see far down the road? Do I take the sharp turn to the right, with no idea of what is out there, or the subtle move to the left with an inkling of what lies ahead? What happens when I reach a dead end? Every crossroad is sacred.

In reflecting on my life at the crossroads, I remember an old *Ziggy* cartoon that goes something like this: as Ziggy drives along in his car he notices a road sign saying, "End of the Old Era." Driving a little farther he spots a second sign, "Beginning of the New Era." Just past this sign is another in big, bold, red letters: "Prepare To Pay Tolls."

A life journey does not unfold in a straight line; the route is often circuitous and sometimes requires an abrupt stop in order to discern the next steps. Recognizing a road that is wrong for me is part of the journey; I don't stay on an uncomfortable road for long. I'll find a crossroad and turn, even when I don't know where the new road leads. And yes, there are tolls to pay.

One of the first times I refused to stay on the wrong road came as I completed my freshman year in college. I had attended a state university in Georgia a few hours from my hometown. The suburban campus felt comfortable to me and, rooming with my best friend, I enjoyed my first taste of real freedom. But I disliked the school and had no clue what I wanted to major in. I withdrew at the end of the spring semester. All of my friends had found the college that fit their needs and I was the only one of our group who was not returning in the fall.

That summer I explored other schools and, while visiting relatives in Tennessee, I stopped by a small liberal arts school, simply because it was on the way to somewhere else. I still remember the walk across the Maryville College campus that hot summer day and my first view of the mountains from the porch of what would be my dorm for the next three years. I knew I had found the sign post for the next road.

Many of my crossroads involve a literal move and are connected with particular places. I often encounter God at the crossroads and on new roads. My first concrete memory of the presence of God was as a seven-year-old attending summer camp in the mountains of eastern North Carolina. This Florida girl was absolutely in awe of the mountains, which were so different from everything I had known. It has continued to be true for me that, when I am removed from my most familiar surroundings, I stop being distracted and God feels so much closer than God does in everyday life. A walk in the winter woods in college experiencing my first snow fall had the same effect as standing on the edge of the Grand Canyon: everything comes into focus, both the vastness and the intimacy of God. Worshiping in a massive European cathedral, visiting the sacred places of the Mayan Indians in the jungle of Guatemala, or reflecting in a small chapel in the Scottish highlands, have inspired the immediate sense of awe from the same source that first touched me in my home church.

Some of my earliest memories are of the church in which I grew up, where I was baptized, confirmed, where I participated in the process for ordination and where most of my family members still attend. First Presbyterian Church in Ocala, Florida is a downtown church and, like most of the historic district that surrounds it, the buildings have a formal historic designation and traditional architecture. I love the sanctuary with its large white columns, rich mahogany pews, magnificent pipe organ and imported stained glass windows.

When I was growing up, there was no such thing as "children's worship" or "extended session." We amused ourselves during worship services eating the Lifesaver candy my mother had in her purse and looking at the colorful scenes in the windows. Much of what I appreciate about worship space and liturgy was formed in those years where, in that big sanctuary, I felt both the otherness of and the *closeness* with God that a familiar place allows.

When my parents presented me for baptism they had no idea that one day I would baptize their grandchildren from that font. When I assisted in washing the communion ware I had no idea that I would one day serve the elements from around that table. When I was one of the speakers presenting the sermon on youth Sunday, my classmates had no idea that I would one day preach from that pulpit. Looking back I see how that nurturing congregation shaped my call to professional ministry in ways none of us could have imagined

I certainly had no idea about the crossroads that would appear after college. I spent the summer traveling through Europe before moving back to my hometown. For the next year I taught school and worked in a church, leading the youth ministry. My parents had always made sure by their examples and their words that my socially and financially privileged upbringing required service to the community and care for others in need. A growing integration of that ethic in my own life pushed me toward a master's degree in social work, and I entered a program the next year at a school in Richmond, Virginia, combining it with a degree in Christian Education. After graduation I found myself at another crossroad.

I moved to Charlotte, North Carolina, with a roommate from school, and began to search for a job. Opportunities for church educators were plentiful and I was offered some good positions in desirable churches, but I wanted one in Charlotte and for several months I kept holding out for a particular church there.

One evening my roommate and I were reading a church publication with the list of all our classmates and where they were working. The phone rang. She answered it, and covering the mouthpiece, whispered the name of the man who was calling for me. It was the chairperson of the search committee of the first church with whom I had interviewed months before; he had offered me a position I did not accept.

"We're still interested in you for the position," he told me. He asked if I would be willing to visit them again and reconsider the offer. I agreed to go, my rational brain telling me that, since the church was near my Florida hometown, I could visit my parents and pick up more of my belongings to bring back to Charlotte with me.

The next day I drove the five hundred miles home. Just as I arrived my roommate called to let me know that the church I had waited for in Charlotte had left a message saying they wanted to offer me that position, the one I coveted. I was in a quandary. I had told this other church I would show up the next day for further conversation. All I really wanted to do was get back in the car and return to North Carolina to begin my career, just as I had planned. I called the Charlotte church and told them where I was and that I did want the position, but I had obligated myself to this other interview.

The next day I drove the two hours to the Florida church, walked in the office door to meet the chair of the committee and that did it. Over dinner that night I accepted the offer they extended. I suddenly knew this was where I wanted to be. The next day I began to arrange a move, and then made all the calls to North Carolina to tell the church I could not accept their offer after all and to tell my friends why I would not be back.

God had let me wander all over the place until the call that I could not ignore became clear. This first job as a Christian Educator challenged me, as my graduate school education collided with real world issues. Three years later, I moved on to a similar position with a church in Knoxville, Tennessee and enjoyed nine years of successful ministry there with a wonderful staff and congregation. It was during this time that the tug on my heart, along with the counsel of family, friends, colleagues, church members and youth with whom I worked, encouraged me to explore the pastorate. I was comfortable serving as a professional Christian educator in a non- ordained role and for years resisted the inner call and would not take seriously the encouragement from others to seek ordination.

As much as I knew this road was right for me, I thought that being ordained would somehow restrict my image of myself. I imagined there were expectations of a pastor that would inhibit me. I had only a few role models of female clergy at the time; none that I admired seemed to have a life that mine could mirror.

I came of age in the 60s and 70s and like many of my peers, found women's liberation to be formative in all aspects of my life. My friends and I believed that we really could "have it all." We would have meaningful careers, be exemplary employees, and change the world on mission trips to faraway lands. We would have a wonderful relationship with the man of our dreams, culminating in a fairy tale wedding. We would spend quality time nurturing our children to be creative and compas- sionate, and as ideal wives we would enjoy our marriages with husbands with whom we would grow together as we supported each other in our personal endeavors. No one mentioned there were tolls to pay. I did not imagine I would have to make choices among all the options available to me or that the choices I made would require sacrifice. Or that other people would make choices for me that I didn't want.

During this time, I discovered that a significant personal relationship with a man who was a minister was not going to work. He supported my going into the ministry but he did not want his wife to be a minister. I now know that I resisted ordination in part because I would have to detach myself from someone who was not going on this journey with me. Until then, my active social life—going to graduate school, working, volunteering and traveling on a moment's notice—had kept me busy and satisfied. But I was ready to move on to something else, to more commitment. I saw that at this point I couldn't have it all, marriage, freedom, and ordination.

Yet, making the decision to complete my Master of Divinity degree came just when I knew it was time to make that move. After tiptoeing around the edge, I finally jumped in to the formal candidacy process. In a matter of days I chose the school, interviewed, applied and was accepted to Columbia Theological Seminary. After having hesitated at the crossroads for a long time, I was suddenly clear and moved ahead swiftly.

As part of the process of candidacy, I moved my church membership back to my home congregation. In doing so I knew that my call—which began when my parents presented me for baptism and was nurtured as I grew up in that church with strong female role models—was the same call that had brought me here now. My independent mother, traditional father, and large extended family were my biggest supporters. It was important for me to come full circle, back home, to the family and church that had given me such a solid foundation. I needed this before embracing the next phase of my journey.

Moving forward I let go of a dream connected to the me I thought I should be so that I could live into the person I was becoming. This crossroad looked different from what I had imagined but provided gifts I would never have received had I not embraced it.

In my first call, as Minister of Word and Sacrament to a congregation in Richmond, Virginia, the Pastor resigned after a year and I became the Acting Head of Staff for the next twelve months. I had been content to preach occasionally but now I was in the pulpit nearly every Sunday. I had not wanted to be the only pastor responsible for congregational care; now I was the one called in the middle of the night by the church members whose teenage daughter had been killed in a car accident; I was responsible for her memorial service. I had not wanted to manage the administrative responsibilities for the church or conduct a stewardship campaign, but I did all that too. The opportunities were not what I would have chosen but were what I needed in order for me to live out my call faithfully. With the support of this congregation, I obtained my Doctor of Ministry degree and, as part of my studies, established new ministries that benefited the church and remain a part of its mission today.

My ministry there ended when the congregation restructured its staffing model and made plans to change the position I held. This decision coincided with my graduation. I thought that my new degree was the ticket to any job I wanted and it did get me through doors I might not have otherwise entered. But it became clear that with the degree I was now competing for jobs on another level, and the competition was stiff.

At the request of the Presbytery, and to be available for other opportunities while continuing my search, I became trained in interim ministry and took a position in a small church community outside Richmond. The members wanted someone to preach every week, visit them in their homes, and moderate the required meetings. I insisted on a month-to-month contract because I didn't think I'd be there long. I had no sense of the culture of this mill town that was struggling to define itself as the mills closed and development went elsewhere.

For me the community may as well have been at the far end of the earth, not forty-five minutes from my Richmond home. The people were theologically conservative and knew I was not; I was careful what I said from the pulpit. As the months went by and I did not find a call that I wanted, I was grateful for these people who trusted me in spite of the fact I was an outsider. My ministry included officiating at baptisms, memorial services, and weddings, requiring an intimacy with the members I had not expected or particularly desired. This was quite an unexpected journey filled with many blessings I will always treasure.

Finally, the congregation found a pastor and I was set to receive a call from a church I was excited about and that I knew wanted me. I was sad to say goodbye to these good folks and yet I was relieved to finally have the search behind me as I readied myself for a move to a new community.

But after months of conversation with this church—culminating in a long weekend visit including house hunting—it turned out I was the church's second choice. I still remember sitting, stunned, in my living room the day I received the news, wondering what I had done wrong.

One full year had gone by since I had left my previous call and completed my doctorate. I had ended conversations with churches and had others end them with me; I believed the timing was perfect for the call I expected to receive. I was so convinced this one was for me that I had no other jobs under consideration. I had to pick myself up, keep paying the mortgage, and start the search all over again. I was exhausted and now regretted the opportunities I had not pursued. It was awkward to run into people from my former Richmond congregation who assumed, as I did, that my degree would have taken me anywhere I wanted to go.

Fortunately, once I got back in the process, many interviews came my way, but nothing happened quickly. Several difficult months passed before a colleague called me and offered me another interim position, this time as an Associate Pastor in a church in a nearby university town. I gratefully accepted. Once again I was commuting some distance to work, this time in the opposite direction, and not just geographically. The two communities could have not been more different. As much as the mill town and conservative little church did not fit me, this liberal, large church in Charlottesville, Virginian at the edge of the mountains was perfect. I happily signed a twelve-month contract and had one of my best years in ministry serving that congregation. I did not mind the drive each day nor did I feel out of my comfort zone, as I had each time I drove to the mill town church.

My confidence returned as I continued to search for another call. And this time things fell into place: after many wonderful months, nearing the end of my contract, the church found someone for the position I held, and I found the position as an Associate Pastor that I had been searching for in a church in Raleigh, North Carolina. All the details of the move fell into place and another road unfolded before me.

Once again, the crossroads hid certain things from view. My new congregation had serious unresolved issues not far beneath the surface, and within a year the other three pastors, along with additional staff and members, had left. As I had done in my former church, I served as the Acting Head of Staff for several months until another pastor arrived. My formal job responsibilities are in adult ministries and congregational care, but my skill set and experience as in interim enabled me to wear the many hats I needed to do my job. Unfortunately, the new pastor had an agenda we did not recognize and motives we were unaware of. At his departure, one more time I was asked to step into another role temporarily, this time with the additional burden that such a high level of anxiety ignites throughout a congregation.

Some of the crossroads in my life I recognized at the time; others I have identified in looking back over the years. The help of good friends, mentors, counselors and others has enabled me to recognize and learn from what I might otherwise have missed. I've discovered through all my calls and crossroads, that I carry too much baggage with me on my journey: physically, emotionally, and spiritually. After my most recent move I had a garage full of furniture and other items that I no longer needed but did not get rid of for months; things I shouldn't even have moved. Emotionally and spiritually the baggage, while burdensome, has often represented a struggle at the crossroads that has been part of the process necessary to move on. Sometimes, perhaps it is a blessing that we can only see so far down the road in front of us, and that the "prepare to pay tolls" sign is obscured.

I am still serving this congregation, where my call continues to unfold; all of us have been shaped but not defined by what has occurred. Appropriate pastoral leadership is now in place and the church is healing, having left a very difficult crossroad behind.

Through each of these experiences my image of God expands as my worldview becomes more enlightened. As questions are resolved, more emerge, and some are still there, held by the tension. When I am thrown off balance, things eventually come into focus but not always at the time and in the way I prefer. I have noticed that it is at the point where I lose my equilibrium that things get recalibrated, often in ways I do not expect. As I become steady again, the clouds part and what was there before is recast in a new light, appropriate to my life at that point. God continues to call me to roads yet unknown.

I am blessed with strong, passionate, vibrant women with whom I have shared this journey, including my mother, close cousins, aunts, and lifelong friends. Joining my journey are newer friends, colleagues, and women in this Rehoboth group.

And the next crossroad? That disorienting holy ground? Is it just ahead or have I a mile, maybe 100, to go before it emerges? What will the next intersection look like? Will a familiar pattern play out or is a new pattern emerging? Nobody knows. But I feel now that I am prepared to pay the toll. At least I hope I am.

Write About:

—Crossroads

—Tolls you have paid

—False starts

—Your family and friends' response to your vocation

—Serving a church with views that are different from your own

—Interim Ministers

—Baggage

Without a Hurt, the Heart is Hollow

Judy Stephens

For me, this time in Rehoboth each month with other women, fellow pilgrims along the way, has been a blessed gift. We are sisters in various ministries, in differing expressions of heart and soul faith, yet united for support, encouragement, and a sharing of our spiritual journeys. At these gatherings I have been able to put aside the denominational pressures (as well as self-imposed critiques) and find in this ecumenical gathering, a common denominator of servant hearts.

Along the way we have read writers who have mentored me and resonated for me. One such person is the Quaker writer, Parker Palmer, who introduced me to the idea of being way open and way closed. This concept reflects the situations in which we find ourselves – not always by choice – and how we choose to respond; at any moment, we can be open or closed to life.

This spacious time with other ministers comes at a time when many of my own colleagues in the United Methodist Church continue to be puzzled, resistant, often distant, and at times downright rejecting of a new order in ordination, instituted in 1996, within our denomination. One would think that by now they would understand and accept the new Order of Deacons. But many elders have not wanted this change and have seen it as an imposition. After all these years, sadly, I feel that they have not fully embraced change.

Let me explain. Before 1996, the position of deacon was a mid-point to becoming an elder, but with the '96 Conference, there are now two distinct orders – deacon and elder – different calls, each with specific duties. Those conference folks could have saved a whole heap of confusion by coming up with another name besides deacon for this new position. Elders are called to Word (Preaching), Service, Order (the administration of the church) and Sacraments. The new Order of Deacon is called to Word (proclaiming, not necessarily preaching) and service (bridging the church and the world.) Two different calls to ministry, both now ordained.

To further confuse matters, those consecrated laity serving in places like Christian education and music who had been Diaconal Ministers were grand-mothered and grand-fathered in. Most of them have benefited from the requirement that deacons and elders' salaries and compensation be comparable. That became a "sticky wicket."

Elders have to itinerate (be open to moving appointments annually); Deacons don't. However, deacons must find their own area in which to serve and then ask the Bishop to approve that appointment. Deacons serve as a bridge, uniting the church with the world. Many serve beyond the local church in their primary appointment, where compensation may be minimal or even non-stipended if it is a new and emerging ministry or a ministry serving the poor and marginalized.

As a layperson, I had served in all levels of leadership in my home church and eventually joined the church staff. When a colleague affirmed my gifts and told me about the new order of deacon, I was elated. The job description fit me. But my senior pastor was less than encouraging, to put it mildly. His reaction: "I don't need you to do that to work for me."

So, as you see, answering a call—especially to that of ordained ministry— has not been easy for me. I've often walked in solitude. I have had some affirmations, but also many questions. I have spent much time in reflection and discernment, looking back at where I have been and also looking down the road to what lies ahead for deacons in the United Methodist Church.

Always, though, I hear and see God in the steps I have taken. Sometimes it's through written messages from others, or maybe words and phrases from scripture or a poem or song. These words become part of me and I have often shared them in the required written reports of the ordination process.

When I was ten, my parents gave me a Bible with this verse inscribed in the flyleaf: "In our prayers for you we always thank God, the Father of our Lord Jesus Christ, for we have heard of your faith in Christ Jesus and of the love that you have for all the saints..." Colossians 1:3-5 (NRSV)

I never asked my mother why she chose that particular passage. But when I read it I am always reminded of God's love and of the faithful prayers—of folks like my parents and other mentors—that have sustained me and brought me back when I was tempted to wander off the path. Maybe that's why Mother chose this verse.

Throughout my faith journey, my mother has been a pivotal influence. She was a firm believer in giving out encouragement, usually in a literary form. She often quoted the Bible and told me about some of her own faith journey and struggles to find a faith that "fit" a life reflecting God's love. Colossians is a collection of letters; Mother wrote letters too, which she has sent to me throughout my life.

Mother had the most intricate, convoluted, drawn-out thoughts, with parenthetical side trips, that were fascinating to read. I often wondered how some of her sentences would look diagrammed on one of those old green chalkboards in the class-rooms of the 60's. She wrote what she felt, with streams of consciousness revealing her thoughts and emotions. I have saved many of her letters, repositories of her wisdom. One such example:

"One of life's great blessings is to be able to think, (I think?)! "About what" is our choice. Right? Right!... So? So be it! In life many different experiences come our way, and we are aware of the frequency of God's love, His goodness, sometimes His

Will. Added to that would be my hope here that I am aware!
I'm going down some roads that are new – so unfamiliar.
Very *smooth* in places, bumpy here and there, and off and on,
full of holes. Passable, but painful to a degree..."

Often I have wished I had shared with my own children some
semblance of the vulnerability and guidance she gave to me.
Like the church writers, Mother wrote to remind me of my faith,
warn against false teachings I would encounter, and to call me
to holy living. An ever-present danger to the Christian
community is the fear that the converts would be led astray by
false teaching, a fear my parents shared. But they should have
known I was a "good girl."

Growing up in the Bible Belt South, I memorized Bible verses
in a program at our school and eventually won a free week at a
non-denominational camp. It was there that I confessed Jesus
Christ as my Savior and Lord; confirmation in the Methodist
tradition would follow soon after. I have had trouble though in
accepting God's unconditional love and grace. The fact that I've
always felt I've had to "earn" things can really wreak havoc
with Prevenient Grace as described by John Wesley, the founder
of Methodism.

In our tradition, Grace—God's unmerited love offered to us
even though we cannot earn nor deserve it—is essential. Wesley
talked about three kinds of grace – Prevenient (coming before
our awareness); Justifying (making things right, salvation which
comes after repentance) and Sanctifying (moving towards
perfection for the rest of our lives). I kept thinking I had to do
something to earn Prevenient grace. I could not accept that I was
"good enough" to deserve it as a child and then later as a wife
and mother.

Something that helped me was the idea of reading the scriptures as if they were written for me. Inserting my name, I could
hear a personal message in what would become a favorite

scripture for me:

> "When you pass through the waters, I am with you, Judy; and
> through the rivers, they shall not overwhelm you; When you
> walk through the fire you shall not be burned, Judy, and the
> flame shall not consume you." Isaiah 43

These are apt lines for me. There have been days of fire and
water in my life, both figuratively and literally. Brought to the
baptismal font by my parents and baptized with the waters of
God's grace as an infant, I was the second-born and oldest
daughter with three siblings. My daddy was a farmer in a
community on the outskirts of a small rural town in North
Carolina called Fuquay-Varina. We were poor, but we never
knew it 'cause Daddy always put money in the collection plate
and Mother always took us shopping once a year for school
clothes. I was part of a hard-working family and, although I
knew I pleased my mother, I still longed to hear from my daddy
that I pleased him. I knew he loved me, but he was not much of
a talker. I wanted to hear him speak those words. I think I had
the same need spiritually—I longed for love from my human
father, grace from my heavenly Father.

I fell in love with, and later married, my high school sweet-
heart, with whom I could share my faith questions. I remember
a special gift Wray gave me after high school graduation. That
baccalaureate sermon has stayed with me throughout life; Wray
had the words engraved on a bracelet for me: "Without a hurt,
the heart is hollow." Those words have stood the test of time and
sustained me during some rough days. I have learned, though,
that it is sometimes through the hurts that we learn the true
depth of love. From feeling way closed, new doorways can open
that we would never have stepped through in a journey of only
way open.

Here's an example. I went off to the University of North

Carolina at Greensboro for a degree in pre-professional social work. Wray and I got married at Christmas just before his last semester at Davidson College. I had thought I would be graduating after exams in January and life looked like "way open" for sure. That January we had one of the biggest snows in remembered history and I was snowed in at our home, out on Lake Norman, some fifteen miles from a main road. I was unable to get off the lake, much less travel the ninety miles to my final exams. So, no exams, and no graduation. There went my plans to teach that last semester. Life felt "way closed."

Times were tough. Wray worked a full-time job and was a full-time student. I didn't have a job. Somehow, we made it through. A commissioned officer, Wray was due to be called up for Vietnam, so after his graduation we headed back to set up house in a little trailer in our hometown where I could be near family while he was gone. In the interim we both took teaching jobs. When Uncle Sam's "call" came, however, Wray's school system requested a delay so he could finish teaching his class for emotionally disturbed children. By then, Vietnam was winding down and he was able to fulfill his commitment through the Army Reserves. We hadn't planned to end up in our hometown. But there we were, somewhat settled.

I taught English for two years and realized I wasn't cut out to be a teacher. There was no way I could do the job as thoroughly as I wanted and still have time left over for a life; when I committed to something I felt I had to work really hard, be as perfect as I could be. After our children began to come along, Wray stepped in to oversee a family-owned business. We were definitely putting down roots in our hometown and soon we found ourselves involved in all levels of leadership in our church life.

I loved being a mom. We had four beautiful children who were born in the same order as my original family: boy, girl, boy, girl. But we were so young when we got married and started having children that we barely had time to learn about each other, not to mention ourselves, before all these responsibilities were upon us. I wanted to carry my weight in the marriage so I took a part-time job with a local newspaper and found I had an insatiable appetite for learning. When I decided to take a class at a nearby university, I rediscovered a world with adults and eagerly embraced a new "way open." That one class led to others and soon I found myself with a master's degree in counselor education. I sought other classes and continued to seek accreditation as a marriage and family therapist. But this "way open" would turn to "way closed" just as I was beginning my last class before taking the state boards.

In the wee hours of the morning of January 18, 1989, we were shocked to hear the yells of our sons followed quickly by the ringing of the phone with a call from my brother telling us to get out, that our house was on fire. In those few minutes our world, as we knew it, was turned upside down. The next days, weeks and months were a difficult road for all our family. For me, just getting through the days was often all I could do. We had lost everything. For insurance purposes, we had to list every item we had ever had, but was no longer there. It felt like we were reliving loss upon loss. It was a time of learning true humility, of receiving from others where before I had always been on the giving end. I confess receiving loads of dropped off hand-me-downs often had me feeling like I was receiving a missionary barrel. I learned a lot about being more appreciative of the little things in life.

There was, however, one very special gift that I received that morning of the devastating fire, for which I will always be grateful. When my parents heard of our loss, they came right away. The first words out of Daddy's mouth when he saw me were, "I love you." There was joy even in the sadness.

Overwhelmed by the emotional necessities of holding a family together, I put my career plans aside. I became despondent and depression set in. I could not make decisions. I didn't want anything new; all I wanted was the old and familiar, a response that would color much of my later life. I still resist change, especially if it is sudden or imposed on me. At times I look longingly to the past before I can press ahead for the future. I often wonder if those behaviors have something to do with having lived through the loss of our house to fire.

When we're faced with loss, especially of this magnitude, and stripped of so much of what we have, we cannot help but see things differently. My priorities shifted dramatically from what I had thought was so important; now I wanted, for sure, to find God's will for my life. When I had accepted Christ as my savior, I had felt the nudge towards missionary service, the only way then that I knew one could be totally committed. I had not followed through. Now, with children and a new course to chart, I was faced again with whether I would be willing to put aside my plans and seek God's plans. I felt inspired by the Celtic spiritual writer and musician, John Bell, who writes in a song called "The Summons" about loving ourselves and allowing ourselves to follow where God calls us to go, even if we know we will be forever changed.

God leads us through and makes all things new—in his Time, not ours. Way open, way closed, way open. Trials with fire had come; trials with water were on the horizon, and my heart was far from hollow. Even though I dislike the idea of multi-tasking, I tried to keep a lot of balls in the air. Saying "No" was never something I did very well; I often took on more than I should have. It's difficult when we want to "have it all" to realize that we have to make choices. We simply can't do it all.

I took a part-time position at our church as Lay Ministry Coordinator and at the same time, worked part-time for the State of North Carolina as a consultant and administrative assistant for the Willie M Review Panel. In the latter position, I worked for a group of professionals who oversaw the provision of education and therapy for children who were neurologically and emotionally impaired and in trouble with the law. I wonder now if I was not trying to be so busy that I wouldn't think or feel. But again life forced feelings.

The enormous power and destructive force of Hurricane Fran hit our area in September of 1996. Trees on our heavily wooded lot snapped like matches; we were flooded for days and without electricity. It was a nightmare for many in our area and also for us. Our older daughter's wedding date was just two weeks following Fran's devastation. Her dream of an outdoor wedding took place amidst the destruction left by massive trees downed by the winds and floods. But we pressed on.

Once again, our family was bombarded with emotional highs and lows slamming against each other. Our son would be married in December, just three months later. Sandwiched in between the weddings, though, my beloved daddy died unexpectedly over Thanksgiving.

The doorways between way open and way closed were swinging wildly in my life. My heart was full from all the hurts I was experiencing. After Christmas I took a month off for some much-needed reflection. It was only then that I faced my feelings: that I was letting God down, as well as others and even myself, by not following through so many times. I began to ponder anew who I really was and what I was really called to be and to do.

The timing of spiritual discernment was providential for me. Again I had to be knocked down, forced to spend time acknowledging my thoughts and feelings. I realized, in a deeper way, how short life really is. I knew that I wanted my life to count. Was I too old now? What could I do with what I had and who I was? It was then that I made the decision to follow God's call into full-time ministry.

United Methodists go to their District Superintendent to learn how to follow their call, but mine (and probably most of them across the country at that time) didn't seem to know what to do with this "new" Order of Deacon concept. Out of frustration, I finally summoned the courage to phone the national office for the new Order of Deacon in Nashville, Tennessee. Sometimes "way open" comes unexpectedly. Rev. Jimmy Carr, the head honcho, just "happened" to answer his phone while his secretary was at lunch; and he just "happened" to be in town over the next few weeks. This just "happened" to be a time when my husband had a business meeting in Nashville. God works in mysterious ways.

After meeting with Reverend Carr, I had a game plan and knew what my District Superintendent needed to do to help me. It turned out that Reverend Carr was one of my very few staunch supporters — way open. I would later, near the end of my ordination process, be given another gift – Jimmy Carr and I washed each other's feet at a closing service for new deacons.

Though it would be a lonely path with little understanding from those around me, I found peace and a kindred spirit from all that I was learning. Having been introduced to John Bell's music, I also discovered how important the Celtic way of life was in my discernment process. Two different opportunities to visit the people of Scotland and Ireland would restore my spirit and give me strength to forge ahead.

We had built a new house but it didn't feel like home to me. I had often heard my mother talk about not feeling like she had a home. Her mother had died from cancer, and being the youngest of sixteen, she was sent to live with an older sibling. Maybe that had something to do with a dream she also had, that of somehow going to Ireland, the homeland of her parents. Gifts also can come unexpectedly.

I was able to take her and my two daughters to Ireland two years before Mother died. I still chuckle as I remember her being frisked in security for the two harmonicas she had tucked away inside her coat; music was as important to her as it was to me.

Mother's health declined when we returned and our lives became a roller coaster ride as she succumbed to congestive heart failure. She went in and out of cardiac failure; I wanted to stay by her side as much as I could. During what turned out to be her final stay in the hospital, I felt an urge to be with her night and day, which was exhausting. "Without a hurt, the heart is hollow."

My heart was full. And I had the gift of holding my mother's hand and singing hymns when she took her last breath and was finally released from all that pain. Words cannot describe the beautiful shaping of her mouth in formless words as the very breath of life seemed to transport her upward and the Spirit left her earthly body. I, who had always been fearful of death, was blessed with that peaceful departure. She was on her way "home" and I received the gift of peace, which enables my ministry now with the dying.

God's call into the ministry was clear, even though it took some creative maneuvering to find seminary classes to fit my lifestyle. I discovered that I could take intensive week classes in Nashville, with United Theological Seminary. I took other classes at Gordon-Conwell Theological Seminary in Charlotte, North Carolina. This alternate route was possible under the new Order of Deacon.

Since I already had a master's degree in a specialized field where I would serve, I only had to take the "Basic 24" required polity and theological courses.

This route was not easy, but I was able to devote my time and effort, again part-time. Hungrily, I soaked up all that I could. I'm not sure I would recommend doing it this way, but for me it worked. I was consumed but I knew where I was heading and I learned to "keep my head above water," a phrase my mother had often used, especially in her written epistles to me.

After spending months writing my ordination papers, I was finally ready to go before the Board of Ordained Ministry. I had no idea how I would do, so it was with surprise that I learned I had passed on the first attempt. There was actually an end to all that preparation. "Way open came quicker than I had expected; I should have known way closed was just around the corner. Even though I had received my call in my home church and wanted to stay there and help, especially in family ministry, the Staff Pastor-Parish Committee had other ideas. The decision of that committee was to rewrite my job description and to tell me that I could apply for it, but that they would not be hiring clergy. I was brought face to face with rejection from the place where I had worked so hard in ministry. The door slammed shut.

Still I could not deny my call. The hurt was immense. It was again from the Celtic Way that I found healing. Once again it would be with God's providential design. I learned of a trip to the Christian community of Iona off the coast of Scotland, a place I had always wanted to visit. I had no idea what kind of group my husband and I would be with; it "just so happened" that we were the only other couple in a group of Biblical story-tellers. We traveled to the Isle of Iona as well as to the modern-day monastery at Northumbria, England. How blessed we were! This holy time apart, again, on a sacred journey enabled healing for me within a community of faith. Again, I received God's acceptance of my call, this time in a Celtic printed verse on the wall in a small crowded living room in the Mother house of that Northumbria community:

May the peace of the Lord Christ go with you,
Wherever He may send you.
May He guide you through the wilderness,
Protect you through the storm.
May He bring you home rejoicing
At the wonders He has shown you,
May He bring you home rejoicing
Once again within our doors.

from Celtic Daily Prayer

I spoke those words, sang them, and wove them into my heart. Wherever He would send me, I would be protected and I would rejoice. The joy that had been missing from lack of affirmation was finding a "home" within my heart. Recognition by others, I would learn, would not come easily for me.

I had grown to love and embrace Celtic spirituality from my first encounter. Even though I was brought up with the understanding that we are all born with a sinful nature, I knew there was something not quite right about that. Celtic spirituality underscores the goodness of God and of all creation and sees the image of God in the heart of each human. That fit with John Wesley's concept of Grace. I also claimed the Celtic saints and angels' presence and protection that I had experienced at critical times, especially at the time of my mother's death.

As I said earlier, deacons must find their own place of ministry and then ask for an appointment from the Bishop. After some time for reflection and for the hurts to heal, I received the wisdom to know what to do. I felt that my gifts and graces could be used in the area of retreat ministry. Due to my insatiable appetite for learning, I had sought certification in retreat ministry and I knew first- hand the power of time apart with God. I wanted to help others cross that threshold into luminal, kairos time.

I asked for, and received, an appointment from the Bishop to the North Carolina United Methodist Camp & Retreat Ministry. This organization, related by faith to the Conference, had just undergone a time of revisioning and had even changed their name from "Camping" to "Retreat Ministry." Since deacons may take a non-stipend position in new and emerging ministries or in working with the poor and marginalized, I decided to serve with them without asking for compensation. I wanted to give of myself because of all that I had received from others. My husband and I prayed for wisdom and I stepped out in faith to serve in a ministry in which he was already serving as executive director.

For five years I served my primary appointment there and had my secondary appointment (as deacons serving in the world are required to do) at Saint Francis United Methodist Church in Cary, North Carolina. There I felt affirmed as I assisted in worship and gave guidance in adult education. Something I had not counted on in both ministries, though, was the emotional impact on my sense of personal worth and integrity from not receiving a salary.

Once again I was struggling with where to draw lines between giving and receiving and not being taken advantage of. My situation became more complicated. I had been diagnosed with rheumatoid arthritis, a debilitating chronic condition with enormous costs especially for drugs and the chemo infusion of Remicade I needed every six weeks. I believe that underlying stress had taken its toll on my body. I needed a paying position with benefits.

Confronting the camping ministry with the fact that retreat ministry, after five years, could no longer be called "new and emerging," I asked for compensation. I was to learn that their plans and mine were not the same. I was asked to go through the process of writing a new job description. It was rejected for compensation. Once again, I felt rejected when I had asked for affirmation. So I turned to St. Francis, my secondary appointment where I had been serving also for five years. With my certification in Christian Education, I offered to serve in a vacant position, only to learn that compensation for that position had been cut, temporarily at least.

What appeared to be another opportunity brought with it a familiar twist. It has been disheartening to learn that all too often people and institutions, even the church, are eager to take willingly what one offers, but oftentimes without compensation.

As I ask for a non-stipend appointment at this church, I am hopeful funding will be found as they see the gifts I bring.

Hindsight is always twenty-twenty. As I look back over my life thus far, I see so many blessings, so much for which to be thankful. I claim Psalm 139, knowing that God has had a purpose for me all along. At times I have listened closely; other times I have tried to do things my way. God has called me to be who I am and to use my gifts and graces in ministry as an ordained deacon at a time of newness for the United Methodist denomination.

Following God's call has brought many challenges, yet I press on in my spiritual journey, I have grown tremendously, particularly through the times of hurt and sorrow. I have found that I need solitude. I also need community. For that special time with my sisters of the faith in Rehoboth, I give thanks.

I continue to be challenged to live in the present moment and trust God to give me the strength and wisdom to step through the doorways ahead. While I hope for affirmation from my peers, I also have a deeper awareness of God's grace.

Write About:

—Embracing change in the church

—Natural disasters

—Prevenient grace

—Doors opening

—Doors closing

—Career plans on hold

—Loss

—Rejection

—Retreat Ministry

Only Grace

Susan Steinberg

A boy slipped his hand into mine on a breezy October morning. Pablo didn't ask and I didn't invite, but suddenly we were holding hands as we walked up the hill to the retreat center in western North Carolina. He was the youngest child in our group of eleven kids, so maybe he needed an extra ounce of security. Or maybe the climb was a bit of a challenge for his small legs. I'll never know what led him to reach for my hand, but I do know that, these days, his silent act of trust is the kind of gesture that affirms my sense of call. I didn't always feel God's call in such fleeting moments. In fact, I haven't always recognized God's call at all.

As I think back to when I first sensed being connected to God—and what God wanted to do through me—I see myself in the eighth-grade, speaking in Quaker meeting, on a bet. I went to a Quaker school from kindergarten through twelfth grade where we were required to attend "meeting" every Thursday morning. As squirmy kids, we endured the forty-five minutes of silence and were relieved when it was over, though as we grew older the mid-week structured quiet offered a welcome respite from the stresses of high school. On this particular day, Julie Rappaport dared me to stand up and say something—contrary to the mores of Quakers, who don't gamble and who wait for the Spirit to move them before speaking. Sitting beside me, Julie kept opening her hand to show me the shiny quarter resting in her palm. If I stood up it would be mine; if not, my loss. Finally, with about five minutes left before we all shook hands to end worship, I decided I really wanted that twenty-five cents. I have no recollection of what I said. I do recall feeling the unexpected sensation, as I spoke, of God's presence.

Many years passed before I considered speaking in front of others about God's love as a full-time job. At our twentieth high school reunion, Lisa Cromley told me she and a few others had made a list when we graduated, predicting what we would all do with our lives. Their prediction for me was minister. If I had known that when I graduated in 1981 I would have laughed out loud.

My family attended a Presbyterian church—my parents met and married in a historic church in downtown Philadelphia, and have been committed to the Presbyterian Church ever since—so I worshipped Protestant-style on Sundays. As much as I came to value the sacred silence of Quaker meeting, I also felt God's presence in the liturgy, music, prayer and proclamation during Sunday morning services. But all the ministers I heard from the pulpit were men, and it never occurred to me that I too could be an ordained worship leader.

The Quaker and Presbyterian communities taught me a variety of ways to live my faith outside the meeting house and sanctuary. When I was in kindergarten, the school organized a peace protest against the war in Vietnam; I'll never forget holding hands with my mother on one side and my younger sister on the other, forming a human circle around our school campus as a gentle rain fell. I wasn't sure what we were doing, exactly, but I understood enough to sense that war was wrong and peace was good; I was proud to stand up for that message. In high school, I babysat for the children of Vietnamese refugees and went on an inner city experience weekend to help paint a poor family's house and attend worship at an African American church. I learned that many people did not have the privileges my own family enjoyed. By opening the doors to the broader world, my school taught me to look for and respect the Quaker "inner light" in whoever I met.

The church taught me a similar belief: we are all created in the image of God. Every week several girls from a nearby foster home came to my Sunday School class. Some of the girls had obvious emotional problems; they were the kind of girls us "normal" kids could easily ridicule. But by including them in the class, the teachers clearly conveyed the message that they had as much right to be there as the rest of us; we are all equal in the eyes of God.

At Wellesley, a women's college outside Boston, I encountered the first ordained clergywoman I had ever met, Chaplain Connie Chandler-Ward. Connie embodied the commitment to contemplation and action that my religious upbringing had ingrained in me. She was all over campus during the week— raising awareness about injustice and war, from apartheid to the nuclear arms race—and in the chapel every Sunday leading the students in prayerful reflection. Connie's life revolved around activism, prayer, and community and she quickly became one of my most formative role models.

Still, I didn't imagine joining the clergy myself. I had other ideas. As I was struggling to figure out my academic major, I asked myself, "What do I want most?" "Peace" is the answer that finally came, thanks to all those years in Quaker school. At that point Wellesley did not have a major in Peace Studies, so I designed my own program.

As I researched what courses would form the core of my major, I learned that Colgate University had a well-designed Peace Studies program; they even had a Peace Studies house, where students lived. I decided I had to go there for my junior year.

Early in that year "abroad" I met Coleman Brown, the Protestant chaplain on campus. Like Connie Chandler-Ward, Coleman lived out his faith in daily life like few people I'd ever met. We used to joke that he only had two suits, one for winter and one for spring, and one pair of shoes, the same old brown hiking boots he wore every day; in fact, we were in awe of his disciplined choices. Like many of my friends, I wanted to be like

Coleman when I grew up. I still do. So I tried to learn as much as I could from him. I took his January term class on the writings of Thomas Merton and in the spring I became co-chair of the campus ministry steering committee.

Because of that role, Coleman asked me to give the "Words of Welcome" during the university-wide Easter morning service. And there it was again: the feeling that as I spoke I was somehow connecting with a voice much larger than my own. But I filed that holy moment away, the way I had the eighth grade dare, not sure what else to do with it—and not curious enough to find out.

I gave all I had to my year at Colgate, with no regrets. But I contracted mononucleosis and was forced to spend the summer resting at home, reckoning with the fact I had pushed myself too hard. Maybe it was the week of the campus ministry dinner followed by the all-night dance marathon for charity followed by another all-nighter writing for "The Colgate News" that did me in, or a solid year full of those kinds of weeks. My mind didn't get the signal but my body let me know I needed to stop. I wish I had learned then to honor my body's cry for attention.

Back at Wellesley I wrote my senior thesis on the Woman's Peace Party, the World War I women's pacifist organization that became the Women's International League for Peace and Freedom (WILPF). My advisor encouraged me to apply for a Watson Fellowship, a grant offered to seniors at a variety of colleges to fund a year's travel outside the United States. My proposal focused on the contemporary incarnation of WILPF, which was celebrating its seventieth anniversary that year, 1985. Was there still a need for a women's-only peace organization? If so, what was its purpose? How was it doing? I proposed to find out.

Even as I applied my intellect to this distinctly secular movement, I remained engaged in the religious life of Wellesley. I volunteered to help the homeless, participated in peace protests and attended Connie's early morning contemplative prayer service. As my senior semester drew to a close, Connie asked me if I would like to preach in the chapel one Sunday. I had no idea what I was doing but said yes and preached something about feminism and faith and the gospel of John. Again I felt that resonance with the holy as I stood up and spoke. I remember Connie telling me that copies of my sermon disappeared from the chapel's literature table. And I remember running into my friend, Rita Mandoli, a few days later.

"Susan!" Rita jumped out of her car to greet me. "Have you ever thought about being a minister? I really think you should!" Her urgency startled me—but didn't change my mind. I hadn't thought about being a minister, and I had other plans.

After the Watson Fellowship, money ran out, in the fall of 1986, I was in San Jose, Costa Rica. The Iran-Contra scandal was just breaking. I had seen some of Nicaragua's impoverished areas, visited families who lived in one-room houses with dirt floors—and children who had rags for clothes and diseases that could easily keep them from growing into adulthood. I couldn't imagine why our country was supporting the contras and sending in our own bombers. What threat did these poor people pose to us?

I decided that my next step would be working to oppose U.S. support of the contra war. Part of that decision came from my outrage at the injustice I'd seen and part came from the religious roots that seemed to be looking for fuller expression in my life. I wanted to make a clearer link between Jesus' command to love our neighbors as ourselves and the way I was spending my time; I wanted to move my faith more to the center of my work.

Through friends I met Martha Honey and Tony Avirgan, well-known American journalists and the plaintiffs in a major lawsuit aimed at exposing the secret deals and drug-for-guns swaps that kept the contras well-funded and well-equipped. Tony and Martha were overwhelmed with all the work and before long they hired me to help with the case—my first real job after graduation.

The lawsuit was known as La Penca case because it hinged on a bombing that occurred at a press conference held by contra leader Eden Pastora in a cabin in the small town of La Penca, Nicaragua. Tony and Martha eventually hired lawyers from the Christic Institute, an "interfaith public policy law center," whose mission was to use lawsuits to heighten public awareness about critical issues.

Christic alleged that a secret team of right-wing Cubans, CIA agents, and Oliver North had acted together over time to plan a series of crimes, from the assassination of John F. Kennedy to the bombing at La Penca. The suit claimed that the bomber was a U.S.-backed contra agent, hired to eliminate Eden Pastora because Pastora's plans did not jibe with the United States' vision for the war.

In the end, the bomber turned out to be a Sandinista and Christic was counter-sued by one of its most well-known defendants and was forced into bankruptcy. But for three years I threw myself into "the case" and into the most radical kind of political work I'd ever done. I believed I had finally found the way to apply the commandment to love our neighbors—the impoverished Nicaraguans we were bombing—to the work I did every day.

Yet I got tired of spending my days researching the hidden activities of our long list of defendants. Though I was drawn to Christic because it was a faith-based non-profit, faith rarely came up in our conversations; and when it did, it was a kind of new age faith I did not recognize. I wanted to hear more about Jesus. I began to consider my next step.

A friend I'd made in Costa Rica, Julie Parker, was doing field work for a Masters of Divinity degree at Union Theological Seminary. She told me repeatedly that I, too, should go to seminary. But law school was my first choice. While I was disillusioned with some lawyers I worked with at Christic, I was deeply inspired by others; I saw myself as a charismatic civil rights attorney. So I took the LSATS and applied to a handful of law schools, places that would never offer a spot to someone with test scores like mine. I deluded myself into thinking that all my hard work for Christic would make up for my other deficiencies.

In fact, the only law school that offered me a chance was Vanderbilt, and even there I was on the waiting list. But after all my thinking about politics and faith, Vanderbilt's joint degree in law and divinity intrigued me. I applied to the Divinity School as well—and got in, with the promise of a two-year scholarship.

"Behold, I have set before you an open door," goes the motto of my Quaker alma mater. I felt at home in the divinity school right away and soon made peace with the fact that as much as I admired civil rights lawyers, God did not intend for me to be one.

Yet I still wasn't sure God intended me to be a pastor. "I do not want to be a minister," I wrote in my journal a few months before the first day of class. I was in the "seeker" category my advisor told me. I had a clear longing to deepen my faith but only the vaguest sense of calling.

That vagueness started to change once I began going to church regularly—something I hadn't done since I graduated from college. Shortly after I arrived in Nashville, in August, 1989, an acquaintance invited me to Second Presbyterian. After four years of travel and spiritual wandering I was looking for a congregation I could stick with for a while. By the grace of God, I was ordained in Second's sanctuary in 1993, almost four years after I first visited.

But I didn't make a straight line from the front door to the chancel. Far from it. It's a long way from the initial step into a church to the steps up to the pulpit, and I wanted to take my time getting there.

My approach changed radically the summer after my first year, when, on a trip for my summer job as a community organizer on the Texas/Mexican border, I rolled one and a half times across a two-lane highway just south of Laredo in my beloved used Honda Accord and walked away with only a scratch on my foot. The Honda was not so lucky—she was totaled—but as I left the wrecking company I remembered the name I had given her: Grace.

God must know I am a literalist. Until then, I believed in salvation by grace on a pleasant, intellectual level. Only after living through the experience of coming within inches of losing my life did I get that being saved is a full-body process that involves letting my own hands off the wheel. In the emergency room, I pondered the precious and short nature of life and considered how much time I'd spent seeking without deciding. By the end of the evening, I felt the keenest sense of urgency about choosing my path I had ever felt.

That urgency was fueled by two other jarring experiences. Just the month before, when I was finishing up the spring semester, my ethics professor came on to me in series of harassing phone calls. I was reeling from that experience, when, as I transitioned from the end of classes to my summer commitment, some guys tried to break into my apartment in the middle of the night. Fortunately, neighbors helped me deal with the situation safely.

But between the attempted robbery and the calls from the professor, I could not wait to drive a thousand miles away from the very place I believed God had led me less than a year before. The accident forced me to examine the fallacy of my deep-seated wish that by distancing myself from my questions and problems they would magically resolve. Yes, the divinity school had welcomed my enrollment; I'd easily found a community of friends, a church I wanted to join, and a way to fund a summer job doing ministry on the border. But was I going to pay any attention to that flicker of the spirit I'd felt in eighth grade or in college? No one could decide that for me. Nor could anyone decide for me to pursue a complaint against the professor. Landing upside down inside a flattened car propelled me into action. I had no more time to waste, it seemed to me.

I went back to Vanderbilt prepared to enter the call process of the Presbyterian Church, and ready to document my troubling interactions with the professor. Yet even as I enjoyed a new clarity of purpose, I also felt burdened by the stress of violation and mistrust as I walked through the divinity school's hallways. When I met with the Dean to discuss my complaint, he told me that "rumors were flying." Who knew about the harassment? How did they find out? The professor was away teaching at Harvard that semester; would he come back? What then?

I chose to limit my time at the school, keeping my eyes down while I was there in order to avoid unspoken questions from other students or professors. In my free time I went to the gym and exhausted myself with long workouts. Then I'd go home and eat hundreds of tortilla chips, washing them down with lots of wine. I couldn't drive away from the pain, but maybe I could run or crunch or drink it out of my body. Much of that second year went by in a blur.

Even as I attempted to push the pain away, though, I found my way towards healthier forms of healing. I discovered support among friends, especially my first-year roommate, who had worked as a counselor for victims of sexual abuse. Thanks to her guidance, and subsequent allegations from other female students that proved the professor harassed not only me but a host of others, I did not feel so alone. I began to notice a quiet voice inside that gave me strength and the beginnings of peace, and I finally started to believe that I had nothing to be ashamed of.

Through all of this, I learned something new about God's presence in my life; I found that with the support of community and the practice of inner attentiveness I could summon the power to stand up for myself—and survive and heal and come back to life from what felt like a kind of death.

Even today, I continue to reflect on how the sexual harassment experience impacted my calling. Though the administration did pursue the harassment charges and made the professor's return to school conditional on certain changes (he never came back), I became more wary of academia, even academic institutions devoted to the study of God. I also developed a mistrust of my own abilities. Did I really earn that A+ in the professor's class, or did he give me that grade because he liked me? Did my work merit the pastor-as-theologian award I received at graduation, or did the deans give it to me because they felt sorry for me? I will never get a clear answer to these questions. They still haunt me.

More than learning to doubt my intellectual prowess, however, I learned that I would be safer if I suppressed a part of myself—my own inner light. In one phone call the professor told me, "Susan, I've imagined what you would be like [in sex]; you are so animated and energetic you would never stop." I found myself sinking more deeply into the reserved part of my personality; expressing my whole self was not worth the risk. As much as I had discovered an untapped inner strength, I moved around in a bushel of fear.

And I had a few methods at hand to deal with fear: running and drinking. The harassment didn't lead me to those habits; it did lead me to take them to new levels. Running five miles wasn't enough; I had to do a marathon. One glass of wine wasn't enough; I had to have three. So went my pattern of "self-care" until well after I left Nashville.

Nowadays I wonder about self-sabotage. With all my efforts to escape fear, did I also block out positive things like God's attempts to get through to me? "Perhaps I am stronger than I think. Perhaps I am afraid of my strength, and turn it against myself, thus making myself weak," Merton says. I can relate. In some ways I feel like I've gambled with God's call over and over, taking it seriously, believing in myself and trusting that God wants to do something through me, then wondering if I'm really cut out to be a minister and questioning my motives for wanting to be affirmed in my pastoral identity.

As much as I've questioned, there have been times when I've been fully certain of my calling. I loved my ordination service at Second Presbyterian in Nashville and I felt completely called to be the Associate Pastor of Westminster Presbyterian Church, in Charlottesville, VA, in 1993.

For seven years that congregation embraced me and taught me and affirmed me. When I fell in love with one of their own, Steve Farmer, though all my training had taught me that such relationships were completely untenable, the congregation celebrated and helped me plan my wedding. When our first child Henry was born two and half months premature, they cared for us all and took up a collection to help us pay our steep medical bills. And when, after our second child Anna was born, I became convinced that God's calling me to be a mother was as important as serving the Church, the congregation sent me off to North Carolina, in 2002, with blessings, fanfare—and a generous purse. Grace upon grace upon grace. I packed up my theology books, pastoral files and clerical robes and put them in storage; I was ready to embrace my new vocation.

Deciding to end my time at Westminster had been a wrenching process, but I was afraid that if I didn't make that decision Henry and Anna would grow up thinking of church as the place that takes mommies away. Already Henry, at age three, said to me between our two Sunday services, "Mommy, you can't go to another service!" When I went to the church on Saturdays to preside at a wedding or work on a sermon, Henry would scold me and insist, "But people don't go to their offices on Saturdays!"

Just as God called me to the ministry, God also called me to be a mother. But making such a radical shift, from full-time ministry to full-time mothering came as a serious challenge, and another season of questioning began. As confident as I had become with my ministerial responsibilities, I was anything but sure of myself with a twenty-two-month-old girl and a three-year-old boy. I was humbled to the core by the new set of demands I faced: toilet training, searching for missing pacifiers, sponging up spilled milk and Rice Krispies. The energy it took me to do all that, day after day and into the night, left me in total awe of childcare workers, single parents, and anyone with more than two children.

When I could step back from the sheer physical labor of caring for the kids, though, I was grateful for the choice I had made to be with them instead of at work. I could be a witness to their growth in ways that never would have been possible; I could be there when significant questions came up, like when Henry would ask, "Why do some people not have houses? Why are there prisons? What does 'dead' mean? Why did Jesus die?" or when they did something that made me laugh out loud, like when Anna painted both of her arms, wrist to shoulder, in purple paint.

Still, after a year of caring for my children as my only job, I decided we could all benefit if I worked for pay part time. I longed to use and be assured of my abilities as a minister. Without the chance to exercise my skills and be part of a community of faith, I felt lost and lonely. I knew God called me to be a mother, but surely not a depressed mother.

After a year as a part-time interim Presbyterian Campus Minister at Duke University, I accepted a part-time job as the Associate Pastor for Children's Ministries at United Church of Chapel Hill. With half-time hours, I could be a minister during the morning and a mother in the afternoon.

As much as this kind of opportunity to balance my personal

and public vocations seemed like a gift from God, when I accepted the position, I did not think of it as a call but more as a transitional job until the kids got older and I found something more substantial. The field of Children's Ministries was secondary to my desire to have a rare twenty-hour-a-week pastoral position. Even as a mother who left full-time ministry because I valued spending more time with my own young kids, I still held on to a hierarchical view of ministry, in which work with children ranks lower than work with adults. I had internalized the unspoken but commonly-held perception that one's value as a pastor is determined by the visibility of the pulpit and the number of adults one serves. I felt I was taking a step down in my career, and I didn't want to stay down for long.

I'm still serving United Church, and my view of Children's Ministries has been transformed. The children have taught me countless sacred truths and have inspired me beyond measure. I have been the grateful recipient of several grants, which have given me the opportunity to engage in creative projects about practicing faith with children—opportunities I never could have foreseen when I started out. I am now convinced that God opened the door to this particular form of ministry not only because it worked with my family's schedule but also because ministering among children and families is the specific mission God has given me during this passage of my life.

Even so, I have gone through serious episodes of uncertainty about my worth and purpose. At age forty, a mid-life crisis touched every part of me and my life. I ran a second marathon, despite constant pain in my hamstrings, and went to physical therapy for months—individual and marital therapy followed.

My mind, body, and spirit ached and I had no idea what God wanted to do with me, except teach me how to pay attention and learn once and for all how to sit with pain instead of running away from it. And help me figure out how to be all of a piece, whole and well, in my own skin. And assure me that I did not need to figure it all out alone.

So when, around this time, a minister friend Marilyn Hein phoned to ask if I would like to lead a Rehoboth group, it felt as if God was calling me — not to a new position, but to a new way of doing ministry where I could balance the responsibilities of pastoral work with the nourishment of honest conversation among peers, shared laughter and tears and, always, the breaking of bread together.

I have been ordained for over fifteen years, and I think I'm finally beginning to understand that as much as my calling is about serving the Church, it is also about being well within my own soul. Rehoboth has helped me tend to this other, more private aspect of God's claim on my life.

"To thine own self be true," a kind professor on my ordination committee advised me. Through regular Sabbath rest, getting my hands in clay and dirt, taking the time to study a strawberry before I eat it, sitting at table with friends who have had their own share of struggles, Rehoboth has given me some of the courage and guidance I need to follow the professor's advice.

I have quit running, and drink only occasionally; though I once believed my life depended on these very habits, I see now how they became parts of the bushel that kept my light in the dark. Instead I have discovered it is the ordinary things that bring me back to myself and connect me with a sacred sense of purpose: writing in my journal, playing with our golden retriever, enjoying laughter-filled dinners with my family. And choosing, every morning, to sit still in a chair by the window, my cat curled up next to me — sitting not because I am in pain, though sometimes I am, but because I long to be present to God.

I used to think I would feel affirmed in my call when a parishioner said "great sermon" on her way out of the sanctuary or when I made it to "the top," but now I notice that I can receive all the affirmation in the world and still feel empty inside. What fills me up are the little gestures, like drinking tea from a mug I crafted in a Rehoboth gathering, or holding hands with a seven-year-old boy who places his trust in me for a few fleeting moments. In those small acts of faith and attentiveness I hear the whisper of God's voice saying, "You are where I want you to be."

Write About:

—Small gestures that affirm your call

—Influential women in your faith journey

—Pushing yourself too hard

— "Behold I have set before you an open door"

—An experience that profoundly changed your life

—Sexual harassment

—Self-sabotage

—destructive habits

—Tension between motherhood and serving a congregation

—The concept of "being well within my own soul"

Contributors

Betty Berghaus is the Associate Pastor for Congregational Care at Westminster Presbyterian Church in Durham, NC. She has served in this position since 1999. She served as a Director of Christian Education for fifteen years in Presbyterian churches in North Carolina, then went to Duke Divinity School, graduating in 1998, before being ordained as a Minister of Word and Sacrament. She has one daughter, Mary, who works with the Center for Disease Control (CDC) in Atlanta.

Cely Chicurel started creating a magical world of animals, dragons, wizards, and castles in her childhood kitchen. She attended Penland and Arrowmont School of Arts and Crafts and has a B.S. from East Tennessee State University majoring in pottery and weaving. For forty years she has been making and selling her fanciful clay creations. Cely also teaches art to children and adults, encouraging them to discover their talents as they play with clay and other art media. In 2001, Cely received a Master of Church Ministry from Duke Divinity School and added spiritual retreats to her growing list of offerings. Today Cely and her husband Bill operate Cely's House, which includes an after school program, weekend creative birthday parties, and summer art camps.

Reverend Caroline Craig Proctor remains an active member of New Hope Presbytery. She received her B.A. from Davidson College and her M. Div. from Duke Divinity School. Her contexts for ministry include hospital settings, local congregations, university campus ministry, and, most recently, a state women's prison. She is a NC licensed massage therapist and body worker and currently studies Chinese medicine. She will incorporate acupuncture and other healing arts into her ministry. She and her husband, Reverend Allen Proctor, live in Raleigh and Asheville, North Carolina. They enjoy hiking, kayaking, and time with friends and family, especially on the Carolina coast and the Blue Ridge mountains.

The Rev. Liz Dowling-Sendor is an Episcopal priest who has served congregations in Durham and Chapel Hill, NC. She is a spiritual director and retreat leader and leads spiritual formation groups at Duke Divinity School and with the Johnson Interns in Chapel Hill. In addition to writing and editing, she offers writing groups through the Resource Center for Women in Ministry in the South, where she serves as Writer in Residence. Before ordination she was a newspaper reporter and magazine editor. Born and reared in Beaufort, SC, she received her A.B. degree from Harvard University and her M.Div. from Duke Divinity School. She has three grown children and enjoys contra-dancing, hiking, singing, and yoga.

Rev. Marilyn Elizabeth Hein, Church Educator, Minister in the Presbyterian Church (USA) holds degrees in Music, Christian Education and Divinity. She served in four churches: in Tennessee, Texas, Florida and Georgia as Church Educator/Musician. For the last twenty years has served the Presbytery of New Hope as Associate Executive Presbyter for Education and Mission. She was ordained to Word and Sacrament in 1997 at age fifty. She lives in Raleigh, NC, loves the beach, books, friends, family, jig saw puzzles, and the thought of retirement.

Carol Henderson teaches writing workshops and coaches writers at every skill level, in the U.S., Europe, and the Middle East. She has published reviews, essays, and features in Woman's Day, The Utne Reader, and other magazines. USA Today called her book, Losing Malcolm: A Mother's Journey

Through Grief, "a redemptive memoir about losing a baby and learning how to live." She is also an award winning newspaper columnist. Henderson's workshops focus on self-expression. She encourages writers to discover their most meaningful material and bring it to the page in their truest voices. Bloomsbury Publishing brought out her most recent volume (2010), an essay collection she developed and co-edited with Mohana Rajakumar, Qatari Voices. www.carolhenderson.com.

Debbie Kirk received her BA from Maryville College Maryville, TN, her MA from Union Presbyterian Seminary in Richmond VA, a Master of Divinity from Columbia Theological Seminary Decatur, GA and her Doctor of Ministry from Union Presbyterian Seminary Richmond, VA. She is a Certified Christian Educator and Minister of Word and Sacrament in the Presbyterian Church (USA). Currently Debbie is serving as Associate Pastor for Spiritual Growth and Nurture at Hudson Memorial Presbyterian Church in Raleigh, NC.

Katie Ricks is the Associate in Ministry at the Church of Reconciliation in Chapel Hill, NC, where she has served since graduating from Columbia Theological Seminary in 2002. She enjoys the opportunity to walk with people throughout their journey of faith, and she is particularly inspired by the witness of children and youth, as they learn and grow. Her ministry focuses on being present with young people as they wrestle and struggle and rejoice with their understanding and experience of God and God's call on their lives. Katie and her partner, Paula, enjoy walking, reading, and playing with their daughter, as well as caring for the animals who also share their home.

Marcia Mount Shoop is an ordained minister in the Presbyterian Church (USA) and serves as the Theologian in Residence at University Presbyterian Church in Chapel Hill. She has her PhD in Religious Studies from Emory University. Marcia is currently the moderator of the national Presbyterian Multicultural Network board and the moderator of the multicultural committee and network in New Hope Presbytery. Her book, *Let the Bones Dance: Embodiment and the Body of Christ* (Westminster John Knox, Sept 2010) is available in bookstores. She teaches, preaches, and leads workshops and retreats in North Carolina and beyond.

Nancy Rozak is a Director of Christian Education at Westminster Presbyterian Church in Durham, NC. She has a BA from the University of Wisconsin and a Masters in Education from National-Louis University, in Evanston, Illinois. She is a Certified Christian Educator in the Presbyterian Church (USA). A thirty-year resident of Lake Forest, Il, Nancy and her husband moved to Durham in 2000 to pursue her career in Christian Education. She teaches adult studies in both the Old and the New Testament and enjoys developing educational programs for children and writing curriculum. The mother of two married daughters, Nancy relishes time with her children and grand-children. Her special interests include writing, needlework, and reading.

Susan Steinberg is an ordained minister in the Presbyterian Church (USA). Since 2002, she has been the Associate Pastor for Children's Ministries at United Church of Chapel Hill, a large United Church of Christ congregation in Chapel Hill, North Carolina. She leads worship, oversees the faith formation programs for children and families, and writes for local and national publications. Her ministry was awarded three grants from Valparaiso Project on the Education and Formation of People in Faith; a Louisville Institute grant funded her sabbatical. Susan grew up in Philadelphia, PA . She received her undergraduate degree from Wellesley College and her Masters of Divinity degree from Vanderbilt Divinity School. She and her husband Steve Farmer have two children.

Judy Stephens and her husband Wray have four children and five grandchildren. She has worked for a local newspaper, taught high school English, worked for the Willie M Review Panel, and served on local church staff. Currently a Deacon in full connection in the NC United Methodist Conference, Judy was one of the first to be ordained under the new order. With certifications in Camp & Retreat Ministries and Christian Education, she has worked for conference camps and is serving at St. Francis UMC in Cary, NC in Discipleship/Family Ministries. She earned an Undergraduate degree in social work from UNC Greensboro and a Master's in Counselor Education from NC State University. Judy has taken classes at several seminaries and specializes in Marriage and Family Therapy.

Afterword

As promised, I'm including some of the prompts and exercises I used with the Rehoboth group. I recommend that you use these starting prompts to "warm up," like stretching before exercising. We opened each group writing session with a prompt about the present moment. I suggest you do the same.

Here are three possibilities. Pick one and write for ten minutes, whatever comes to you.

Starting Places
1. What matters now?
2. What are you carrying? In your heart, soul, on your shoulders, in your purse?
3. What's in front of you? Be literal if it suits you—a table and a piece of paper and a pen... Go from there. Or try: What's in front of you in your life right now?

Energy Surges and Zaps
Draw a line down the middle of a blank piece of paper. On one side, make a plus sign (+) and on the other a minus (-). Under the plus sign, list what gives you energy. Under the minus sign, what depletes your energy. Next pick an item from each list and write in more detail about it. Finally, write about how you might increase the energy boosters—and decrease the energy drainers—in your life.

Where I'm From
The poem, "Where I'm From," by George Ella Lyon (you can find it easily online) is an excellent prompt to use when a group is getting to know each other. The poem inspires writers to uncover specific, concrete images from their lives. Often they turn up phrases and imagery they've never before explored or expressed.

Sensory Alert: Writing Outdoors

I invited the women to go outdoors, sit quietly, then write from all five of their senses. "What are you hearing, seeing, smelling, etc?" Next I invited them to write from the point of view of a tree, a cloud, a stone. Before sending them out, I read them "Stone" a poem by Charles Simic.

What Would She Think?

I suggested they write a journal entry. "Write what you might have written when you were 13 years old."

Beliefs and Superstitions

I read them an excerpt from the book, *A Leak in the Heart*, by Faye Moscovitz, about the author's mother's superstitions. Then I read a humorous passage from Annie Dillard's *An American Childhood* describing a child's superstitions about nuns and Catholics. "What beliefs and superstitions ruled your house when you were growing up?" I asked. "Both overt and covert. Make a list, then write about one or two items on your list." When they finished, I invited them to write about their own beliefs and superstitions—not then but now.

Ambush Prompt

During one session I handed each woman a random photograph from a magazine and an unrelated newspaper headline. One of my students calls these "ambush prompts." You have no idea what you're going to get and you can't choose. One might get a photo of city children playing in the water of an open fire hydrant and a headline reading: "All he wants is a little respect." Another photo might show a young man in sunglasses, behind the wheel of a car, and the headline might be "When Europe Wept." "Write a story using these two sources," I said. This prompt invites writers to explore fiction or to use these random images and words to give fresh meaning to a personal experience. It never fails to stretch writers. (If you want to use this prompt, start collecting photographs or art prints and clip headlines from newspapers.)

Call Poems

As the women began thinking more specifically about their call narratives, I offered more poems. Here are a few that evoked deep responses:

"I Used to Be But Now I'm" by Ted Berrigan, from *The Collected Poems of Ted Barrigan*

"Wild Geese," by Mary Oliver, from *Dream Work*

"An Open Door," by Richard Reichard, from *This Brightness*

"Snowdrops," by Louise Gluck, from *The Wild Iris*

Look for poems that express strong images and feelings but avoid cliches. Read the poem aloud and invite participants to write—not an analysis of the poem but memories and ideas the poem inspires. "Start with a line that sticks with you," I might say. Sometimes I cut up lines from a poem and let people draw one from a hat to use as a writing prompt.

Close to Call

In one meeting, I had the women respond to writing prompts that were more specific to the idea of call:

* Write about a time when you felt God close.
* When did you first feel the call to ministry?
* How has your call evolved and changed over the years?

Other Ideas

Prompts are everywhere. Write about everyday objects, a daily routine in list form, a place that no longer is, an empty wine bottle. One time I brought in an old wooden box with drawers and containers, set it in the middle of the table, and invited the women to write about it. They were amazed at the myriad associations and feelings the box evoked—memories of a childhood dollhouse, telling secrets, a container for human ashes, leaving home. You'll be delighted at what the simplest prompt can elicit.

Writing Group Guidelines

If you put a writing group together, one person should facilitate the sessions, giving the prompts and calling out "time" when the writing period is over. Whoever takes this role should also write and read and be part of the group. Pick a group member who is blessed with a good sense of boundaries and experience leading groups.

The facilitator should:

— Always inform the group how long they will be writing. Let them know that if they finish early they can sit and meditate—or write about something else.
— Give the group a two-minute warning that the writing time is drawing to a close. (Fifteen minutes is a good writing time for many prompts.)
— Ask who would like to read and make sure the same person doesn't always read first.
— Invite a short discussion about the writing they have just heard. What's strong? What stands out?
— Invite the group to write in response to the reading they have just heard.
— Important: participants should not respond to someone else's writing by talking about their own experience of the subject. Rather, invite them to write their experience. Keep the discussion focused on the reader's work.
— Post the **C.L.E.A.N.** guidelines where everyone can see them:

Confidentiality. Everything that is read and discussed stays in the group. This is essential for building trust and allowing people the freedom and ease to write deeply.

Listen devoutly to each other's readings. Comment on what's strong and memorable in the writing; avoid negative observations. If something triggers a memory for you, write it down and use it as a prompt for yourself later. Keep the focus positive and on the reader.

Expand. Let yourself experiment with forms you've never tried before. Write fiction, dialogue, a poem, from your pet's point of view, or about yourself in the third person. We hope you will feel deepened and enriched by the writing and by sharing your words with others.

Avoid criticizing anyone's writing. This is all fresh first-draft material. Criticism inhibits the flow of ideas and destroys trust.

No one has to read what they write.

Good luck on your writing journey and don't hesitate to get in touch. You can contact us through my website, www.carolhenderson.com
We look forward to hearing from you.

Further Reading

Books about Writing

Schneider, Pat. *Writing Alone and With Others*. Oxford: Oxford University Press, 2003.

Rainer, Tristine. *The New Diary: How to use a journal for self guidance and expanded creativity*. Los Angeles: Tarcher, 1978.

Goldberg, Natalie. *Writing Down the Bones: Freeing the Writer Within*. Boston: Shambala, 2005.

DeSalvo, Louise. *Writing as a Way of Healing: How Telling Our Stories Transforms Our Lives*. Boston: Beacon Press, 2000.

Caneron, Julia. *The Artist's Way: A Spiritual Path to Higher Creativity*. New York: Putnam,1992.

Memoirs on Call

Copenhaver, Martin and Lillian Daniel. *This Odd and Wondrous Calling*. Grand Rapids: Eerdmans Publishing Company, 2009.

Craddock, Fred. *Reflections on My Call to Preach*. Atlanta: Chalice Press, 2009.

Hister, Richard and Kelli Walker-Jones. *Know Your Story and Lead With It*. Herndon, VA: The Alban Institute, 2009.

Keppel, Nancy Peeler and Jeanette Stokes, eds. *God Speaks, Women Respond*. Cleveland: United Church Press, 2004.

Lamott, Anne. *Traveling Mercies*. New York: Anchor Books, 2000.

Lischer, Richard. *Open Secrets*. New York: Broadway Books, 2002.

Miles, Sara. *Take This Bread*. New York: Ballantine Books, 2008.

Norris, Kathleen. *Dakota*. New York: Houghton Mifflin Harcourt, 2001.

Taylor, Barbara Brown. *An Altar in the World*. San Francisco: HarperOne, 2010.

Circle Books

Circle is a symbol of infinity and unity. It's part of a growing list of imprints, including o-books.net and zero-books.net.

Circle Books aims to publish books in Christian spirituality that are fresh, accessible, and stimulating.

Our books are available in all good English language bookstores worldwide. If you can't find the book on the shelves, then ask your bookstore to order it for you, quoting the ISBN and title. Or, you can order online—all major online retail sites carry our titles.

To see our list of titles, please view www.Circle-Books.com, growing by 80 titles per year.

Authors can learn more about our proposal process by going to our website and clicking on Your Company > Submissions.

We define Christian spirituality as the relationship between the self and its sense of the transcendent or sacred, which issues in literary and artistic expression, community, social activism, and practices. A wide range of disciplines within the field of religious studies can be called upon, including history, narrative studies, philosophy, theology, sociology, and psychology. Interfaith in approach, Circle Books fosters creative dialogue with non-Christian traditions.

And tune into MySpiritRadio.com for our book review radio show, hosted by June-Elleni Laine, where you can listen to authors discussing their books.

MySpiritRadio